COACH
TRANSITION PLAY

Full Sessions from the Tactics of Simeone, Guardiola, Klopp, Mourinho & Ranieri

WRITTEN BY

MICHAIL TSOKAKTSIDIS

PUBLISHED BY

CW00643333

COACHING TRANSITION PLAY

Full Sessions from the Tactics of Simeone, Guardiola, Klopp, Mourinho & Ranieri

First Published February 2017 by SoccerTutor.com

info@soccertutor.com | www.SoccerTutor.com

UK: 0208 1234 007 | **US:** (305) 767 4443 | **ROTW:** +44 208 1234 007
ISBN: 978-1-910491-12-6

Author
Michail Tsokaktsidis © 2017

Edited by
Alex Fitzgerald - SoccerTutor.com

Cover Design by
Alex Macrides, Think Out Of The Box Ltd.
Email: design@thinkootb.com Tel: +44 (0) 208 144 3550

Diagrams
Diagram designs by SoccerTutor.com. All the diagrams in this book have been created using SoccerTutor.com Tactics Manager Software available from **www.SoccerTutor.com**

Note: While every effort has been made to ensure the technical accuracy of the content of this book, neither the author nor publishers can accept any responsibility for any injury or loss sustained as a result of the use of this material.

CONTENTS

MEET THE AUTHOR

MICHAIL TSOKAKTSIDIS

- **UEFA 'A' Coaching Licence**

- **Bachelor Degree in Physical & Sports Education**
  (Specialising in Soccer Conditioning).

- **10 years as a professional player in Greece** (Doxa Dramas, Iltex Likoi (WOLVES), Agrotikos Asteras, Ethnikos K., Pandramaikos and Olimpiakos Volou).

- **Author of Jose Mourinho Attacking Sessions** (2013)

- **Author of Spain Attacking Sessions** (2014)

m.tsokaktsidis@gmail.com

During my career I won 6 championships with 5 different teams. At the age of 29 I stopped playing and completed my studies in fitness conditioning and football coaching. I was also a student of the UEFA coaching schools (H.F.F. in Greece) and I am a fully certified UEFA 'A' licence coach.

I started my coaching career in youth football for 3 years and for the last 6 years I have been a head coach at F.C. Doxa Dramas (professional Greek team) and 3 different semi-professional teams in Greece (winning 2 championships). Football is my main focus in life and I have a deep passion for coaching. From very early I was interested in studying training methods as well as observing and analysing how they are successfully applied.

For this book I wanted to create and present specific content for coaches to improve their training sessions in one of the most important phases of the game in modern football - the transition phases. I believe that transition play is crucial for the final outcome of all games. The efficiency and effectiveness of teams in both phases (transition from attack to defence and vice versa) can distinguish a good team from a very good or great team.

The best teams of the last decade have been successful in large part due to their ability in the transition phases. A prime example of that is Pep Guardiola's Barcelona team who applied the '6 second rule' in the transition from attack to

defence. Another is Jürgen Klopp's Borussia Dortmund and Liverpool teams with their 'Gegenpressing' and very fast break attacks. Other recent examples include Mourinho's Real Madrid, Inter and Chelsea teams, along with Simeone's Atlético Madrid and Claudio Ranieri with Leicester City.

We split the content into the transition from defence to attack and the transition from attack to defence. All possible situations encountered in a football match in these phases of the game are split into sub-categories of the 3 basic zones - low, middle and high.

In the first part of the book we have an analysis of the theoretical part which includes what the transition phases are, how important they are and what decisive role they play. We also look at the teams and the coaches that the book's ideas are based on and how we can organise an effective game model and playing style - what are the key aspects we must have to achieve success?

At the beginning of each session, we present analysis of a top coach and team in the transition phase. We then present specific practices to train for that exact tactical situation. These practices make up full progressive training sessions with detailed and clear instructions.

I believe that teams which have been prepared well tactically for these game situations can be very effective and successful, while also producing an attractive and exciting style of play with a high tempo, speed and energy.

8

COACHING FORMAT

1. TACTICAL SITUATION AND ANALYSIS

2. FULL TRAINING SESSION FROM THE TACTICAL SITUATION

- Functional Practices / Transition Games

- Game Situations

- Rules, Coaching Points, Variations & Progressions (if applicable)

KEY

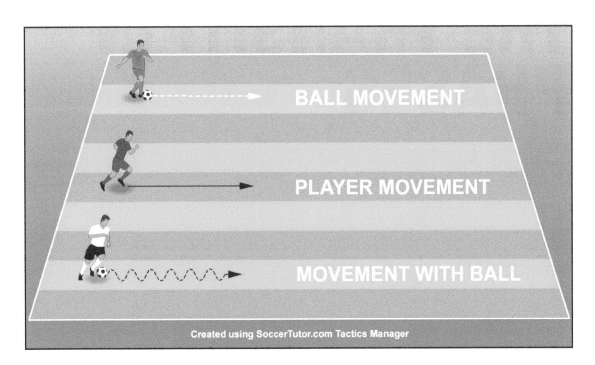

Created using SoccerTutor.com Tactics Manager

CHAPTER 1

THE TRANSITION PHASES

THE TRANSITION PHASES

In every football match, whether it be at amateur level, professional level or even the UEFA Champions League final, we can see the same specific and repeated game situations within the transition phases of the game.

THE 2 TRANSITION PHASES:

- **Transition from Defence to Attack:** The moment a team wins the ball from their opponents, we enter the transition from defence to attack (positive transition).

- **Transition from Attack to Defence:** The moment a team loses the ball to their opponents, we enter the transition from attack to defence (negative transition).

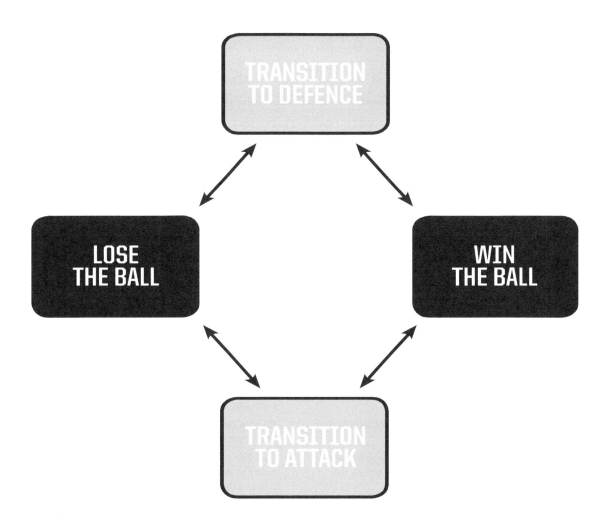

THE LOW, MIDDLE AND HIGH ZONES

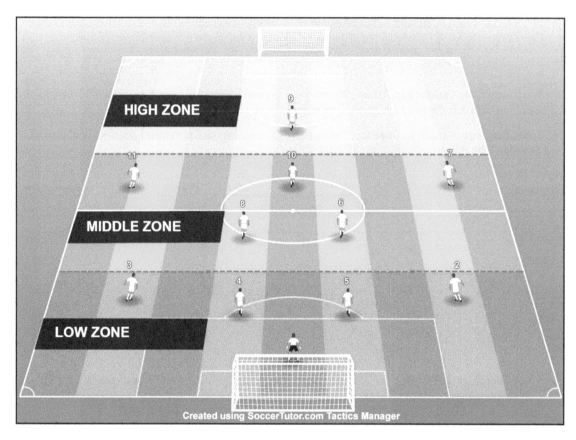

Created using SoccerTutor.com Tactics Manager

For this book, we have divided the chapters by which zone the transition starts in. There are 3 zones/thirds - high, middle and low. The zone always refers to the team we are focussing on.

In the *'Transition from Defence to Attack'* section, the zone refers to where that team wins the ball. In the *'Transition from Attack to Defence'* section, the zone refers to where that team loses the ball:

TRANSITION FROM DEFENCE TO ATTACK

- **High Zone** - The team win the ball high up the pitch and close to goal, then attack.

- **Middle Zone** - The team win the ball in the middle of the pitch and then attack.

- **Low Zone** - The team win the ball deep in their own half and far from the opponent's goal, then attack.

TRANSITION FROM ATTACK TO DEFENCE

- **High Zone** - The team lose the ball high up the pitch and must defend.

- **Middle Zone** - The team lose the ball in the middle of the pitch and must defend.

- **Low Zone** - The team lose the ball deep in their own half and must defend with their opponents close to their goal.

HOW IMPORTANT ARE THE TRANSITION PHASES?

Football is a game of constant turnovers of possession. We always have one team defending, trying to win back possession of the ball. The other team is therefore in the attacking phase, trying to create goal scoring opportunities. These transitions happen continuously throughout a game and can happen extremely quickly.

Whether a team will be successful or not is largely down to whether they are capable of exploiting the unbalanced defence of the opposition when they win the ball and whether they can close down space and limit the options of the opposition when they lose the ball. In the modern game, the faster you are able to react as a team in the transition phases, the more successful you will be!

TRANSITION FROM DEFENCE TO ATTACK

After winning the ball, a team should look to exploit the tactical situation as quickly as possible. It is important to move the ball forward before the opposition are able to close down the ball carrier and mark the potential receivers of the next pass.

The transition from defence to attack requires quick reactions, anticipation, technical accuracy, visual awareness of the space to play into, intelligent movement and good decision making. This means that the players need to demonstrate physical speed and speed of thought.

The aim is to train your teams in the transition from defence to attack at high intensity so they learn to play at high speeds. The faster they are able to make this transition, the more successful the team will be.

TRANSITION FROM ATTACK TO DEFENCE

After losing the ball, it is important to apply immediate pressure to the new ball carrier before he can get his head up to be able to dribble or pass forward. This should be done with the player that lost the ball and at least one more player closing the area around the ball zone. The rest of the players make sure to mark the potential receivers and block the passing lanes.

The players need to react immediately after losing possession and anticipate the positioning/movements of their opponents. This has to be worked on in training sessions to make sure that the defensive movements are coordinated as a team, with good cohesion and communication. As like the positive transition, the negative transition (from attack to defence) needs to be done at a high intensity and speed - making sure that the opposition are unable to exploit the team's lack of balance and launch a successful fast break attack.

TOP COACHES IN THE TRANSITION PHASES

There are many teams and many coaches who have put particular emphasis on the transition phase of the game and have been able to achieve great success in football.

The most important coaches who have had the most influence in recent years, with both their ideas and their implementation of their training philosophy in the transition phase, have been:

- **Diego Simeone**
  (Atlético Madrid)

- **Pep Guardiola**
  (Barcelona, Bayern Munich and Manchester City)

- **Jürgen Klopp**
  (Borussia Dortmund and Liverpool)

- **Jose Mourinho**
  (Inter Milan, Real Madrid, Chelsea and Man Utd)

- **Claudio Ranieri**
  (Leicester City)

On the following pages, each coach's ideas and tactics are presented.

DIEGO SIMEONE'S TACTICS IN THE TRANSITION FROM DEFENCE TO ATTACK

Diego Simeone

"I am always enthusiastic and when I came, I said I wanted to rediscover the essence of the club: An Atlético team that was always aggressive, intense, competitive, counter-attacking and fast… I think that's what we've been giving."

Real Madrid and Barcelona are two of the three richest football clubs in the world. However, since Diego Simeone has taken charge of Atlético Madrid, they have competed with these two powerhouses with a fraction of the budget. This is down to how well drilled Simeone's team are. This is also largely due to their impressive tactics and performances in the transition from defence to attack.

Atlético Madrid won La Liga and reached the Champions League final in 2014. They are still competing at the top of Spanish and European football, only finishing 3 points off the top of La Liga in 2016 and reaching the Champions League final for the second time in three seasons.

Atlético Madrid have used a variety of formations and players in Simeone's time at the club but the underlying philosophy remains the same - to defend, be aggressive and score on the counter. In the big games, such as Real Madrid or Barcelona, Simeone often chooses to use the 4-4-2 formation. They are willing to cede possession, sitting behind the ball and denying space to the opposition. When they win the ball, they then launch very quick and decisive counter attacks.

When in the defensive phase, the Atlético players stay close to each other within a compact formation, making sure not to leave any gaps to play through and limit the space between the defensive and midfield lines.

If the opposition play the ball out wide, the whole Atlético team shifts over as a unit. They will then press the ball, and if the opposition player is able to beat one man, he will then be faced with another and another. This requires high energy and intensity which Simeone gets from his team. As Atlético are set up in a compact unit, they often have many players around the ball, which makes it easier to win a loose ball and then quickly play it forwards.

When in the transition from defence to attack, Simeone's Atlético always look to play forward quickly, either exploiting the space left out wide or in the middle, depending on the particular opponent and their specific weaknesses. They then have very quick support players who make deep runs to get in behind the opposition's defensive lines to receive and create goal scoring opportunities.

Antoine Griezmann is a key player for Simeone's Atlético Madrid in the transition from defence to attack. Atlético would always choose to play through the middle if they could, as they play with a narrow 4-4-2 against the toughest opposition. Griezmann could either drop short to help with the quick combination play, offering a forward passing option for the midfield, or he could make runs in behind, utilising his pace in behind the opposition's defence. He would often be able to get to the ball and create an opportunity himself, or hold the ball up and bring others into play.

Example Analysis of Diego Simoene's Atlético Madrid Team: **Positive Transition**

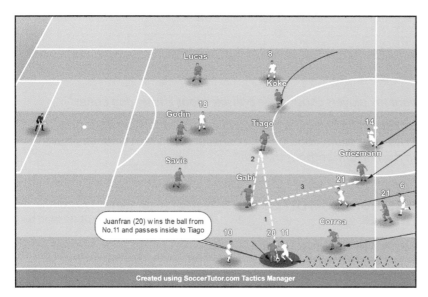

In this example, the opposition's left winger (11) is running forward with the ball. Atlético Madrid's right back Juanfran (20) is able to tackle him and pass inside to the central midfielder Tiago. This starts a transition from defence to attack.

Tiago passes to Gabi who then passes to the forward Griezmann who has dropped back to receive.

Griezmann (7) turns and runs forward with the ball. There is a lot of space in the opposition half to exploit.

Gameiro (21) makes a run in front of Griezmann and receives a forward pass. In the meantime, Correa makes an overlapping run in the space on the right. Gameiro plays a well timed pass in behind for Correa who runs into the penalty area and shoots at goal.

Atletico's would most often attack quickly in the positive transition and exploit the space in behind their opponents.

15

PEP GUARDIOLA'S TACTICS IN THE TRANSITION PHASES

Pep Guardiola

"I want my players chasing the ball like (dogs chase) dog bones."

"'You cannot be brilliant when you disappear when you don't have the ball. It's impossible. Football is a connection between what you have with the ball and without the ball."

We have used content from 'FC Barcelona Training Sessions' (written by Athanasios Terzis) to provide analysis of Pep Guardiola's tactics in this section.

TRANSITION FROM DEFENCE TO ATTACK

During the defensive phase, Barca looked to force the ball towards the sidelines where pressing was easier. Once they regained possession, the players reacted quickly to move into free space and provide options.

When Barca regained possession near the sidelines and there was superiority in numbers in their favour, the team would attack down that same flank. If there was not a numerical advantage, the team looked to move the ball towards the centre where the man in possession had many options.

When Barca regained possession in the centre, the new ball carrier had the opportunity to pass the ball forward and attack through the centre. The wingers would make diagonal runs to receive.

If a forward pass could not be played, the ball was usually directed towards the sidelines. In order for this option to be available, the quick reaction of the full backs to create width was needed.

Example Analysis of Pep Guardiola's Barcelona Team: Positive Transition

The ball is won near the sideline by the left forward Villa (7).

As Villa is in a 1v1 duel with the full back, he directs the ball towards Messi (10) who provides a passing option towards the centre.

Messi then has 2 passing options in the large gap left in the centre (one being to shoot at goal).

TRANSITION FROM ATTACK TO DEFENCE

Pep Guardiola, who perhaps coached the most attractive and efficient team of all time at Barcelona, based his philosophy on the idea that his teams must use high pressure immediately after losing the ball, with the objective to isolate the opponent, preventing him from dribbling the ball forward and blocking any potential passing options. This tactic would force the opponent to directly or indirectly lose the ball for his team. This tactic in the transition from attack to defence became known as the '6 second negative transition' or the '6 second rule'.

Under Pep Guardiola, Barca's main aim during the negative transition was the immediate regaining of possession. To achieve this there was always a safety player near the ball zone, as well as a quick reaction from all the players.

The safety player would also have the appropriate position in order to apply immediate pressure on the ball by reducing the available time and space for the man in possession.

In the example shown below in the diagram, the safety player is Xavi (6) who passes the ball towards Pedro (17). The opposition's midfielder contests Pedro and wins possession. Xavi (the safety player) then moves quickly to close him down and the other Barca players also react quickly to move towards the ball zone.

Example Analysis of Pep Guardiola's Barcelona Team: **Negative Transition**

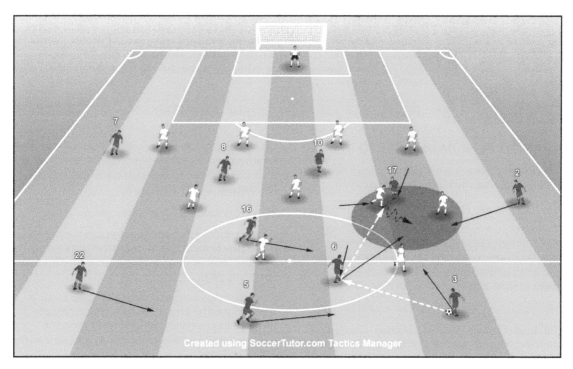

Barcelona's main aim during the negative transition was the immediate regaining of possession. The safety player (6) would have the appropriate position to reduce the available time and space for the new man in possession.

The opposition's central midfielder wins the ball. Xavi (No.6 - the safety player) moves quickly to close him down and the other Barca players also react quickly to converge and move towards the ball zone. For the negative transition to be successful, all players take part.

JÜRGEN KLOPP'S TACTICS IN THE TRANSITION PHASES

Jürgen Klopp

"The best moment to win the ball is immediately after your team just lost it. The opponent is still looking for orientation where to pass the ball. He will have taken his eyes off the game to make his tackle or interception and he will have expended energy. Both make him vulnerable."

"Football is about emotion and speed. It's a transition game".

"If you win the ball back high up the pitch and close to the goal, it is only one pass away a really good opportunity most of the time. No playmaker in the world can be as good as a good counter-pressing situation."

We have used content from 'Jürgen Klopp's Attacking and Defending Tactics' (written by Athanasios Terzis) to provide analysis of Jürgen Klopp's tactics in this section.

Jürgen Klopp left his mark in Germany with his Borussia Dortmund team. The philosophy was based on intense and direct pressure of their opponents (similar to Pep Guardiola's Barcelona team) which was called 'Gegenpressing', but also on the immediate fast direct combination game in the transition from defence to attack. Klopp has now implemented this same style successfully with Liverpool in the English Premier League.

TRANSITION FROM DEFENCE TO ATTACK

Jürgen Klopp's tactics in the transition from defence to attack can be classified into 3 main parts:

1. Direct Positive Transition

The direct positive transition is carried out when the ball is intercepted high enough up the pitch and there is no pressure on the ball carrier. The attackers can make forward movements into the free spaces in order to receive a pass on the move, into their path.

2. Indirect Positive Transition with a Forward Pass

This kind of indirect positive transition is carried out after regaining possession high up the pitch, but because there is pressure on the ball, the forward pass towards the free space is not possible.

The most advanced forward has to move towards an available passing lane in order to provide a passing option for the man in possession. This provides the opportunity to pass the ball forward (but not towards

the free space). After the forward pass there is usually a back pass to one of the midfielders and because an open ball situation is created, there is usually then a forward pass into the free space.

3. Indirect Positive Transition with a Switch of Play

When neither the forward pass towards the free space or the pass towards the advanced forward's feet is possible, the man in possession plays a horizontal pass (switching play).

This switching play pass is usually directed towards the full back who breaks forward immediately after the team have regained possession. This kind of positive transition takes more time to achieve than the other two kinds.

We have an example of an 'Indirect Positive Transition with a Switch of Play' on the next page. This is taken from analysis of Jürgen Klopp's Borussia Dortmund team.

Indirect Positive Transition with a Switch of Play

The Borussia Dortmund No.10 Mkhitaryan is on the strong side and applies pressure high up the pitch.

The defensive midfielder Kehl (5) intercepts the forward pass from the red centre back (4).

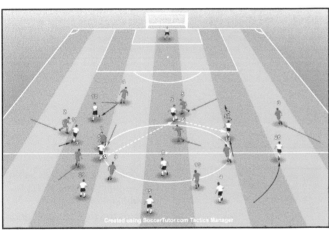

Kehl (5) is put under immediate pressure by red No.8, while both No.2 and No.6 shift across towards the ball area. This blocks the forward pass towards Mkhitaryan (10), so Kehl passes to Lewandowski (9) in the centre. Lewandowski then plays a first time pass into the path of Aubameyang (17) who makes a forward run.

The right back Piszczek (26) also makes a run forward to join the attack.

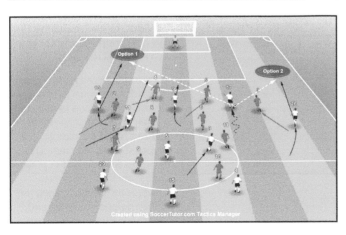

Aubameyang (17) moves forward with the ball and No.9, No.10 and No.11 move forward to receive the final pass.

The right back Piszczek (26) moves further forward on the right to provide a passing option in case a final ball into the penalty area cannot be played (option 2).

The rest of the players move into positions which ensure balance, good shape and safety at the back.

TRANSITION FROM ATTACK TO DEFENCE

During the negative transition (from attack to defence) Jürgen Klopp's teams apply immediate pressure on the ball most of the time, to try and regain possession as quickly as possible.

In order for a team to be able to regain possession immediately, several elements are essential when carrying out the attacking phase:

1. Retaining superiority in numbers at the back during the possession phase.
2. Retaining balance in midfield.
3. Retaining balance near the sidelines to cover for the forward moving full back.
4. Retaining a safety player at all times.

Example Analysis of Jürgen Klopp's Borussia Dortmund Team:

Creating a 3 Man Defence with the Full Back Dropping Back on the Weak Side

The Dortmund centre back Sokratis (25) makes the forward pass, but the opposition's midfielder No.6 intercepts the ball.

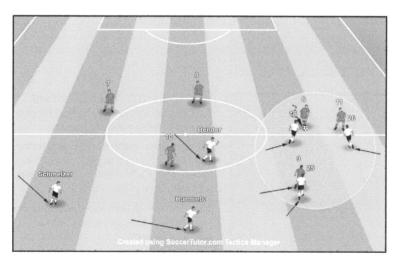

The defensive midfielder Sahin (18) applies pressure on No.6 immediately, forcing him towards the sideline and Bender (6) drops to cover. The right back Piszczek (26) converges towards the centre and marks his direct opponent No.11 who is a potential receiver.

As the striker (red No.9) moves towards a potential passing lane, Sokratis (25) moves to mark him closely so he can aggressively contest him if the pass is directed there. Hummels (15) drops to cover Sokratis's position and Schmelzer (29) moves towards the centre to keep the 3 man defence compact and retain superiority in numbers.

JOSE MOURINHO'S TACTICS IN THE TRANSITION PHASES

Jose Mourinho

"What tactical trends do you see at the top level of the game? Transitions have become crucial. When the opponent is organised defensively it is very difficult to score. The moment the opponent loses the ball can be the time to exploit the opportunity of someone being out of position. Similarly when we lose the ball we must react immediately."

"Everybody says that set plays win most games but I think it is more about transitions."

We have used content from 'Jose Mourinho's Real Madrid: A Tactical Analysis' (written by Athanasios Terzis) to provide analysis of Jose Mourinho's tactics in this section.

Jose Mourinho is a coach who has had big success in 4 different countries and with 4 different teams in the transition phases. Perhaps more so than Guardiola and Klopp, he combines both the transition from defence to attack and the transition from attack to defence very effectively. His view on the transition to defence is that the focus should be on the quick return of the players behind and around the ball. In the transition to attack, Mourinho focusses on specific attacks, working to exploit his team's strongest points (as individuals and as a group) against the weaknesses of their opponents.

TRANSITION FROM DEFENCE TO ATTACK

During the positive transition, Real Madrid were said to be the most successful team in the world under Jose Mourinho. Having players like Ronaldo, Benzema, Di Maria and Ozil who could exploit the free spaces and make quality passes meant Mourinho prepared a team which could counter attack very effectively.

When Madrid won the ball in the midfield and the opposition blocked off all the available forward and diagonal passing lanes, the team mainly sought to move the ball towards the weak side of their opponents in order to exploit the potential free spaces. If there was no available space to exploit, the team then tried to retain possession.

When a forward or diagonal pass was possible, the team could very easily reach the opposition's penalty area and create chances. When Real defended deep and close to their own penalty area, Ronaldo's poor defensive positioning high up the pitch gave the team a great advantage in attack. Ronaldo's positioning

usually led to a 3 v 3 situation and plenty of available space to be exploited in the opposition's half.

The main weapon for Real Madrid, like every other team Jose Mourinho has managed was the transition from defence to attack. In this phase Real were the best team in Europe. Depending on the opponent, how they defended and where they lost ball, Real Madrid would find the quickest and most effective solutions to enter the penalty area and score a goal.

TRANSITION FROM DEFENCE TO ATTACK IN THE LOW ZONE

Jose Mourinho's Real Madrid played very intelligently in this phase - they would often have many players in the low zone and only 1 or 2 players near the halfway line. Their objective was to make a transition from defence to attack very quickly using forward passes into space and they would look to exploit their faster and higher quality players in 2 v 2 or 1 v 1 situations. In these situations, the time they would take to finish

their counter attack (from the moment they won the ball) would be 9-12 seconds.

In many cases during the transition from the low zone, Real attacked with 4 players who would look to play the ball wide at the correct time, to fully exploit the space on the weak side of their opponents. In these situations, the counter attacks were faster than the previous ones and more entertaining, with the attacks finishing within 7-9 seconds.

In the third scenario, when the opposition had lots of players in the centre, 1 or 2 Real players would move up to provide support, very quickly coming from the back and the sides (usually the left or right forward) to call for the ball in the space in front of them. The wide forwards took up better positions than the defenders in this situation, using their speed to assist or score a goal. The average time to finish these counter attacks was around 10 seconds.

When Mourinho's Real Madrid won possession in the low zone, the team would often look to dribble the ball up to the defensive line (causing the opposition to become unbalanced) and use delayed passes in behind. In these cases the opposition usually had 4 or 5 players behind the ball, but not many quick players tracking back to support - so Real would enter a transition to attack in a 4 v 4 or 5 v 5 situation.

The objective was to dribble up to the penalty area and then pass to a teammate free in space who was normally on the flank. They would then use low crosses in between the last defenders and goalkeeper to score.

TRANSITION FROM DEFENCE TO ATTACK IN THE MIDDLE ZONE

1. If Mourinho's Madrid won the ball in the centre and a Real player ran forward with the ball on the break, the opposition usually only had 4 players behind the ball and their defence would be a large distance away from the other players. Real would enter into a transition to attack in a 4 v 4 situation and the objective for the player with the ball was to dribble up to the defensive line and for the other players to make diagonal runs in behind to receive the ball and score.

2. Many teams who lost possession in the middle zone kept a high defensive line, but Real Madrid were extremely strong in this scenario and could recognise the situation immediately, knowing

exactly how to exploit it. The objective was to utilise their players' speed and attack the space in behind the opposition's defensive line. The player who won the ball would make a quick pass, making sure to retain possession and the second player would likely make the final pass into space for an oncoming runner.

3. We also had situations where the opposition were unbalanced when they lost possession and had many players in front of the ball, with only 2 or 3 players behind the ball. In this case Mourinho's Real Madrid team would launch a fast break attack with an overload, like 2 (+1) v 2 or 3 (+1) v 3. This was an easy situation for a team of Real's calibre to exploit in the transition from defence to attack. The timing of the upcoming runner from deep (+1) and the timing of the pass into space for this spare man was key to Real's success in these situations (creating a numerical advantage in the high zone).

TRANSITION FROM DEFENCE TO ATTACK IN THE HIGH ZONE

Here we analyse what happened when Real Madrid went into a transition from defence to attack in the high zone and very close to the opposition's penalty area.

This would normally occur when Real were attacking using safe possession and were trying to find attacking solutions against an opponent with an organised defence in the high zone and lost the ball.

They would immediately move to press the player in possession, denying them time and space. This was done at a very high tempo to create a successful transition from defence to attack in the high zone.

The objective in this situation was to exploit the imbalance in the defensive line that did not have time to react and close the gaps between their players.

The player who won the ball would look to immediately play a forward pass to a teammate in a better position close to the penalty area. The attack would normally be concluded in a maximum of 6 seconds.

Example Analysis of Jose Mourinho's Real Madrid Team: **Positive Transition**

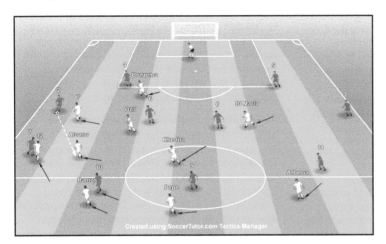

In this example, Real Madrid's defensive midfielder Xabi Alonso wins the ball in midfield by intercepting a pass from the opposition's right back.

As the opposing players react quickly and block the potential forward passing options, Xabi Alonso passes across to his central midfield partner Khedira.

The right back Arbeloa has moved forward into the free space on the weak side, so Khedira plays a long pass to him (switching play).

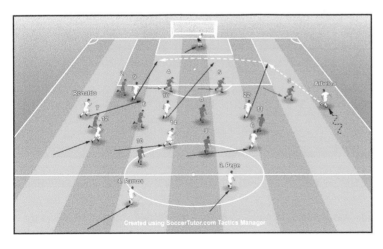

Arbeloa has plenty of free space and takes advantage by running forward with the ball.

Di Maria (22) makes an inside run to outnumber the opposition's left back (3) with Arbeloa and receives in behind.

Benzema (9) and Ozil (10) make runs into the box and Ronaldo (7) moves to the edge of the box for a potential cut back from Di Maria.

The other Real players shift across to support the attack and prepare for the potential loss of possession.

TRANSITION FROM ATTACK TO DEFENCE

Under Mourinho's guidance, Real Madrid became very effective during both the negative and positive transitions. During the negative transition (from attack to defence), Mourinho's main aim is to apply immediate pressure on the ball carrier as soon as possession is lost. To be successful during this phase of play, the team has to remain compact, balanced and have a safety player in the appropriate position to apply pressure on the ball. The success of the team in this particular phase of play is key for them to dominate possession throughout their matches.

The safety player was usually in a supporting position behind the man in possession and would be available for a potential pass back or to apply immediate pressure on the ball if possession was lost. The defensive midfielder Alonso was by far the most important player for Real Madrid during the negative transitions. Alonso had the role of the safety player

in most of the team's negative transitions and could analyse tactical situations extremely quickly.

For Madrid's style of play to be effective, Alonso was the key. He would always take up the appropriate positions, reacting well to varying tactical situations that arose on the pitch. His positional sense and defensive abilities often led his team to regain possession immediately after losing it.

An important element of Real Madrid's negative and positive transition play was the full backs' appropriate positioning against the opposing winger. The positioning of the full backs helped the team to retain its balance and be effective during the transitions. When the ball was lost, the full backs would attempt to take up effective defensive positions against the opposing wingers immediately. When the team regained possession, the full backs moved into advanced positions, ready to receive a potential forward pass free of marking.

Example Analysis of Jose Mourinho's Real Madrid Team: **Negative Transition**

In this situation, the defensive midfielder Khedira's attempted pass towards Ozil is intercepted by the opposing central midfielder No.6.

As in most situations for Real Madrid under Mourinho, Xabi Alonso was the safety player and the first player to close down the new ball carrier.

The 2 full backs Marcelo and Arbeloa move towards the centre to take up goal side positions against the wingers (7 & 11).

Alonso (14) and Khedira (6) are the 2 safety players who move to block No.6's available passing options.

As Real Madrid converged and closed off the space, they would create a numerical advantage around the ball zone, and would often win the ball back very quickly.

CLAUDIO RANIERI'S TACTICS IN THE TRANSITION FROM DEFENCE TO ATTACK

Claudio Ranieri

"Today, some complain that Leicester lose too many balls. But that's only natural, when your team plays at the speed of light."

"I give my strikers freedom to attack and cut across the lines, as long as we immediately return to a 4-4-2 as soon as the ball is lost."

Claudio Ranieri's Leicester team relied on speed of thought and speed of movement. Their unprecedented success in winning the English Premier League (2016) was largely due to the intensity and efficiency of their players and the simplicity of their tactics in the transition from defence to attack.

When defending, Leicester would form 2 solid lines of 4 and would keep close distances between each other. Okazaki (the second striker) would also work very hard in the defensive phase, making sure to put pressure on the ball or track back to provide cover for teammates. It was important to remain compact and deny the opposition space. They were very difficult to break down and their centre backs (Morgan and Huth)

were very strong at defending crosses and set pieces. Vardy would remain high up for a potential transition to attack.

When Leicester won the ball from the opposition and made a transition from defence to attack, they would look to attack at a high pace and directly towards goal.

Leicester always wanted to utilise the speed of their attackers by passing in behind the opposition's defence, in between the 2 centre backs or in between a centre back and full back. Their most effective tactic was to play long passes in behind the opposition defence very quickly, making full use of Vardy's pace advantage over the opposition's defenders.

Example Analysis of Claudio Ranieri's Leicester City Team: Positive Transition

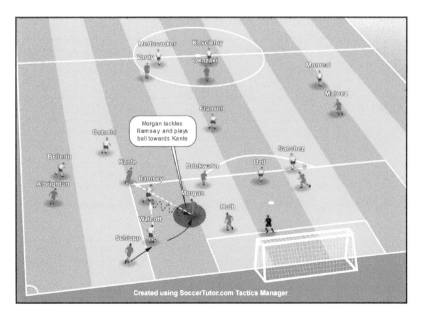

Created using SoccerTutor.com Tactics Manager

In this example Arsenal are attacking inside Leicester's penalty area. Walcott passes back to Ramsey who tries to dribble the ball inside.

Morgan is able to tackle Ramsey and the ball ends up with Kante who then runs forward with the ball.

When Ranieri's Leicester won the ball in the low zone, they would often look to play direct passes to exploit the space in behind the opposition's defence and exploit the speed of their striker Vardy.

Created using SoccerTutor.com Tactics Manager

Kante carries the ball forward and passes to his central midfield partner Drinkwater. As Leicester's plan in this situation was to exploit the space in behind the opposition's defence, Vardy, Okazaki (20) and Mahrez all make forward runs which the Arsenal defenders have to follow.

Vardy is very quick and was a threat via long passes in behind throughout the 2015/2016 Premier League season. It was often Drinkwater who would play the passes as he has great long range accuracy.

In this example, Vardy makes a forward run and Drinkwater plays a long pass into the space on the left. Vardy is much quicker than the Arsenal centre back Mertesacker (4) and is able to get to the ball well ahead of his marker, control the ball with his head, dribble inside and finish in the far corner.

This was a typical Leicester counter attack and a huge part of their championship winning season. As was often the case, Okazaki (20) and Mahrez were also sprinting forward to provide support.

CHAPTER 2

HOW TO COACH AND PLAY IN THE TRANSITION PHASES

CREATING A GAME MODEL

- How can you train for the transition phases?
- How can you organise your training of transition play better?
- What is the best way to coach transition play?

To answer these questions we must first look at what the appropriate training is. My personal view is that good training has to be game realistic (taken from the game and for the game).

This creates substantial training and gives us the results that we want - it is the most effective method to organise your team and work on specific match scenarios. This helps our players and the team to apply exactly what we want from them on the pitch.

- How can we make sure our training is game realistic? What is our guide?

For each training session we need to focus on meeting our targets we want to apply on the pitch. The objective creates the practices, but the talent of the players and the coach's ability is what defines and differentiates the training. The game itself is the guide, but not any game, it must be our own game - how we want to play from the moment we lose the ball and how we want to play from the moment that we win the ball. Before creating specific practices, we must first create our own 'Game Model' which will be our guide for the tactics and training of our team (see diagram below).

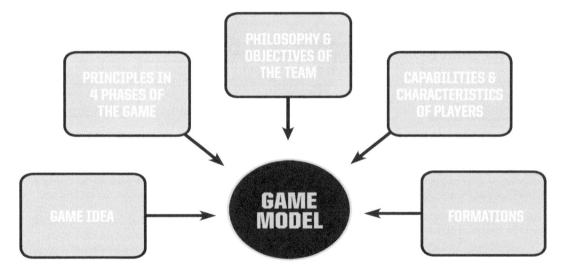

Game Idea: How do we want to play football? This includes the style of play in every phase of the game.

Principles in 4 Phases of the Game: Those who want to succeed in all 4 phases of the game start with the fundamentals and basic principles, working through sub-principles step by step. Football is played in specific areas and specific zones, so the training should not be general and unspecific - it must be specific and concrete.

Philosophy & Objectives of the Team: The purpose, vision, mission, short-term goals, medium-term goals and long-term goals of the team.

Capabilities & Characteristics of the Players: What players do we have in our team? What tactical, technical and physical skills do they have? What are their strengths and weaknesses? Analysis of all of these elements can help us to create a path to follow in our work and in relation to the transition phases.

Formations: With this in our minds, we must find the appropriate formations that can best utilise our players to achieve the team goals and be directly linked to the basic principles of our game model. We need to specifically focus on transition play and become more effective and efficient.

PHILOSOPHY, OBJECTIVES OF THE TEAM AND ADOPTING THE GAME MODEL

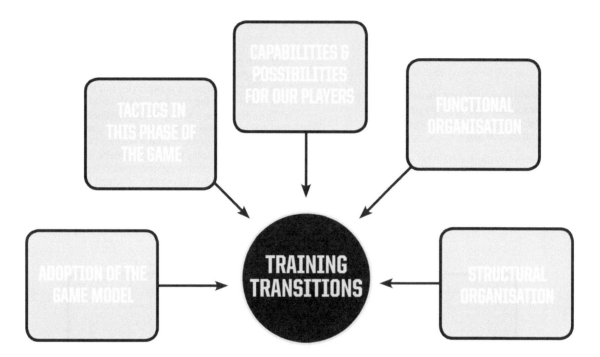

Adoption of the Game Model: Adoption and implementation of the game model which should be decided upon after analysing the factors presented on the previous page 'Creating a Game Model'.

Tactics in this Phase of the Game: Our specific idea about the transition phases - how do we want to play in these phases of the game?

We need to combine all the elements that we want to characterise us as individuals and as a team when winning or losing the ball.

Capabilities & Possibilities for Our Players: We have to take the analysis of the 'Capabilities and Characteristics' seriously and then proceed with the design of where and how we want to behave when we lose the ball and when we win it.

Functional Organisation: Here we include all the specific details. We must work out in which zone (low, middle or high) we will we start our defence, how we will react when we win the ball and how we will recover the ball in the negative transition. This includes how to act when we lose the ball as individuals, as a small group and as a full team, depending on the zone we are playing in.

Structural Organisation: All the previous information should be used to form our defensive and attacking formations against the formation of our opponents. The emphasis is on exploiting our strengths in relation to the weaknesses of the opposition.

COACHING TRANSITION PLAY

High Press, Win the Ball + Fast Break Attack with Support Players

In this situation Barcelona win possession near the sideline. The left back Abidal (22) wins the ball and leaves the opposition's wide midfielder behind him, so a 2 v 1 situation is created on the flank.

David Villa (7) moves towards the available space on the flank, while Messi (10) provides an available passing option. The ball can be passed either directly (option 1) or through Messi (option 2) to Villa (7). In both ways, the left forward (Villa) receives the ball in space high up on the flank.

Messi (10) and Pedro (17) make supporting runs to receive the final ball inside the penalty area and score.

ASSESSMENT:

When the opposition were trying to build up play, Pep Guardiola's Barcelona team always wanted to force the ball towards the sidelines. Their pressing was then easy to apply and the options for the ball carrier were limited. As soon as they regained possession, the players reacted quickly to move towards free space and provide passing options.

When Pep Guardiola's team regained possession near the sidelines and they had superiority in numbers around the ball zone, the team would attack down that same flank, as shown in the diagram example above.

TRANSITION TRAINING: WHAT IS NEEDED?

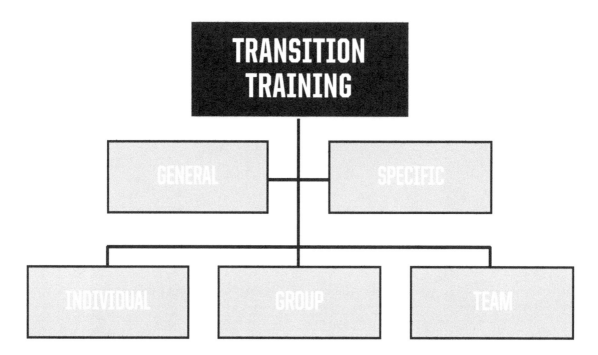

General Training

In general training practices (individual, group and as a team) we focus on improving the starting points for these tactical situations. We also work on quick reactions and decision making, combined with the efficiency and effectiveness of our work against the opposition.

Specific Training

In specific training practices we apply all these ideas into game scenarios versus active opponents using formations, positioning within zones of the pitch and directional play. This is more realistic and tailored to competitive games and the real situations that the players will encounter.

What is Needed?

The transitions themselves are situations that require intensity, rhythm, energy and speed (in all its forms) and above all, quick decision making. That is why they are the most exciting phases during a football match.

These changing game situations contain combination play, individuality, aggression and determination. So it is very natural for the training of such situations to involve intensity, energy, change of pace and direction, and speed/power training. This training should be done on the days when we can work with high intensity.

Our basic and most important goal should be to produce players, groups and teams which understand, decide and act very quickly and effectively. And of course, this must be done faster than the opponent!

CREATING A "THINKING PLAYER"

To train transition play well, specialised and specific coaching is needed with intense workouts. This is the only way to produce a team with exceptional rhythm, good decision making and effectiveness on the pitch, showing more speed and enthusiasm than the opposition.

In the practices and sessions provided in this book we have a continuous and progressive flow to our training, with high rhythm and intensity. This results in a very quick improvement of the players' tactical and technical level.

It is in training where you can imprint ideas and gain the interest of the players, which then improves the required speed and efficiency of their decision making - creating the 'Thinking Player'.

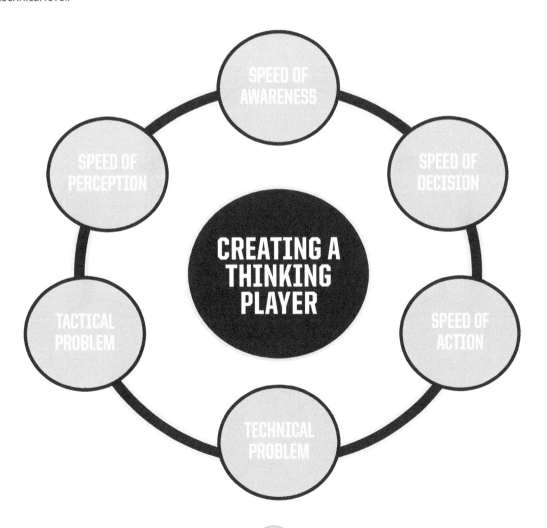

CREATING A PRACTICE

Pitch Dimensions

The necessary dimensions of the created space in which we will perform the practice to have the greatest possible benefit.

Duration

The total and optimum working time of the practice.

Number of Players

The total number of players required for the execution of the practice.

Objective of Practice

What is the main objective? What do we want to work on and improve in this practice?

Methods

The coaching and training methods to follow so the execution of the practice give us the desired results.

Coaching Points

What are the key coaching points to which we should focus our players for the correct execution of the practice? At what points should we emphasise these and offer feedback to our players?

Rules & Directions

All rules and directions under which players have to work in during the practice, with the aim to drive them towards the desired objective and development.

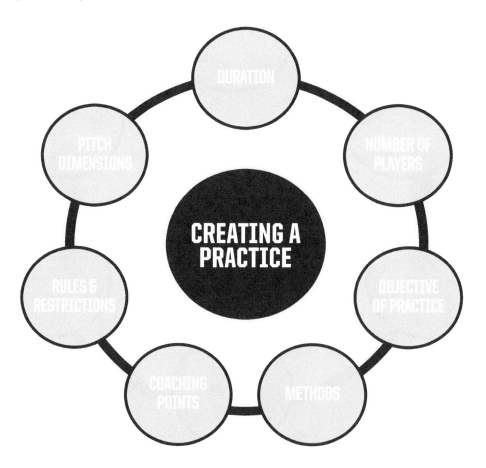

Continuous Transition to Defence / Attack in a Dynamic 8 v 8 Game

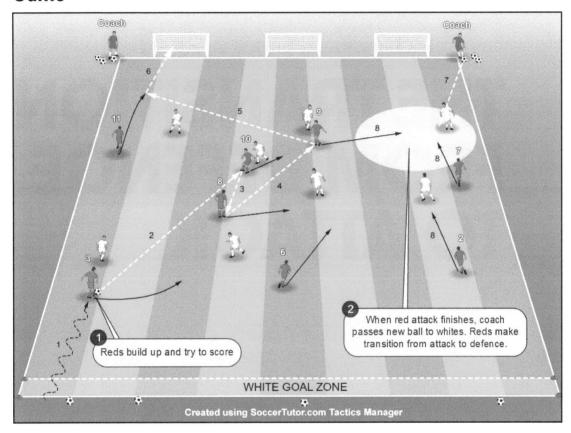

Description

In a 40 x 60 yard area we have 3 mini goals at one end and a goal line at the other end. We play 8 v 8 (reds in a 2-4-2 / whites in a 4-4 formation). There are 2 coaches/players on the outside with lots of footballs.

Scenario 1 (Diagram): One red player dribbles the ball from the goal line and the first objective for the red team is to try and score in one of the 3 mini goals (1 point for either side goal & 2 points for the middle one). Once their attack is finished, the coach then immediately passes a new ball to the white team. The reds second objective is to then make a quick transition to defence, win the ball and attack for a second time (transition to attack).

The whites aim to score by dribbling through the end goal line (or passing & receiving within it) to score 2 points. When the white team's attack is finished, another red player gets a new ball from the goal line and the practice continues in the same way.

Scenario 2: The red team continuously defend in the first phase. A coach passes to a white player and the red team apply a high press trying to win the ball and then counter attack at pace. When the red counter attack is finished, the other coach passes a new ball to another white player and the reds must switch the point of their defence and apply a new high press, win the ball and launch a counter attack again.

THE TRANSITION FROM DEFENCE TO ATTACK

CHAPTER 3

TECHNICAL & TACTICAL REQUIREMENTS IN THE TRANSITION FROM DEFENCE TO ATTACK

COACHING THE TRANSITION FROM DEFENCE TO ATTACK

In this phase of the game we should first and foremost think about where we start our defence, which zone of the pitch we apply our pressure, and finally in which zone we have the best chance to pass quickly from defence to attack.

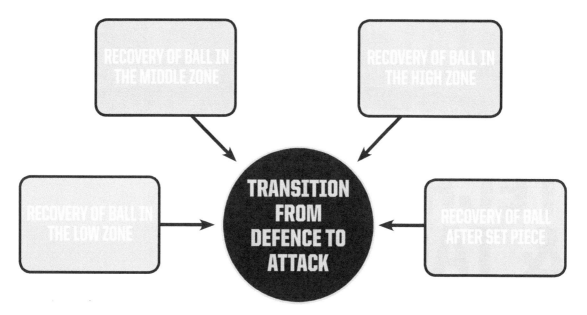

Based on this, every coach should be targeting his team's training on the recovery of the ball in specific zones.

We then work on how he want to attack from that point, based on what kind of players we have in our team and what kind of players the opposition have. We must utilise the individual strengths of our players and our strengths as a group, against the weaknesses of our opponents.

TRANSITION FROM DEFENCE TO ATTACK FLOW CHART

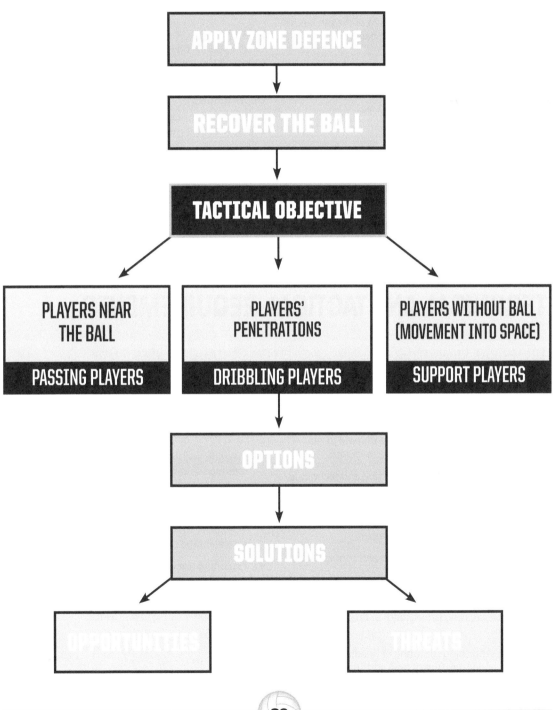

Apply Zone Defence

The zone we decide to apply our defensive press in a specific match depends on our tactical/technical characteristics and formation against our opponent.

Recover the Ball

We must decide which zone and area of the pitch our team should try to win/recover the ball.

Tactical Objective

What are the tactical objectives that we have in this situation as individuals, as a group and as a whole team?

Decision Making

- The player in possession who should pass - where, how, when?

- The player in possession who should drive forward with the ball (dribbling) - where, how, when?

- The player without the ball - what movement should he make? Should he run forward, move to support, create space for himself or for teammates? - Where, how, when?

Options

What are the basic objectives and options in all of these situations and how can we exploit them?

Solutions

What solutions do we have and how can we use them to exploit this situation? (We can provide the players with 1-3 solutions for each situation in training).

Opportunities

What are the opportunities in these tactical situations and how can we exploit them to get the best results?

Threats

What are the threats we must pay attention to which the opposition may be able to exploit?

TECHNICAL AND TACTICAL REQUIREMENTS

TECHNICAL REQUIREMENTS

- When the opposition try to make passes in behind or cross the ball into the box, we don't want our players to clear the ball aimlessly or off the pitch. We want them to clear the ball towards a teammate or into space for a teammate to run onto, so we can quickly attack (transition).

- Correct body shape when pressing and technique when tackling or intercepting the ball.

- Accurate passes - to feet or into space.

- Weight, timing and speed of passes.

- Excellent directional first touch and control of the ball.

- Fast dribbling with close control of the ball.

- Accurate crossing (short, long) or final pass into the box.

- Accurate finishing (shooting or heading) in all forms, under pressure of time and space.

TACTICAL REQUIREMENTS

- Effective defence (individually, as a group and as a team).

- Creating and exploiting space (from the player who won the ball or another player).

- Creating and exploiting a numerical advantage or overload situation.

- Dribble the ball at the opposition to unbalance them.

- The ability to work effectively with a numerical disadvantage or with equal numbers.

- Exploiting the weak side and the weakness of the opposition's defensive line.

- Exploiting the space and time before the opposition are able to reorganise.

CHAPTER 4

TRANSITION FROM DEFENCE TO ATTACK IN THE LOW ZONE

TRANSITION FROM DEFENCE TO ATTACK IN THE LOW ZONE

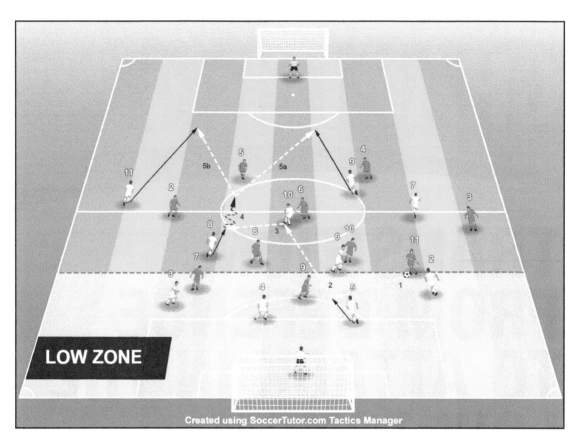

LOW ZONE

Created using SoccerTutor.com Tactics Manager

For this book, we have divided the chapters by which zone the transition starts in. There are 3 zones:

1. Low Zone

2. **Middle Zone**

3. **High Zone**

This diagram shows an example of a team that has won the ball in the low zone. In this situation, the white team have players behind the ball when defending. To win the ball, they need to limit their opponent's time/space, block potential passing options and demonstrate good anticipation.

The red team are attacking and have entered the final third, trying to find solutions to get in behind the defence and score. The white centre back No.5 intercepts the left winger's (11) pass towards the striker (9) near the edge of the penalty area.

The centre back (5) immediately passes forward to No.10 which immediately leaves 5 red players behind the ball and takes them out of the game. No.10 plays a first time pass into the path of No.8, who runs forward with the ball. The winger (11) and the striker (9) make runs into the space out wide and in the centre respectively.

The red centre back (5) is forced to close down white No.8 who then has 2 very good passing options in behind the defensive line, both of which would end up with a player through on goal, and with a great chance to score.

COACHING TRANSITION PLAY

What is the Tactical Situation?

- The opposition have many players high up and in our half of the pitch.

- Our team would often be defending with many players behind the ball.

- Our defenders have a numerical superiority or equality of numbers against their opponents.

- There is a long distance to the opposition's goal.

- We usually only have 1-2 attacking solutions at the top of the attacking line.

- The 1-2 players at the top of the attacking line can be supported by 1-3 players (maximum) running up from the back.

- Our attackers have equality of numbers or a numerical disadvantage against their opponents. There could also be an overload situation e.g. 2 (+1) v 2.

- There is a lot of free space to exploit in the opposition half.

What Objectives Should We Have?

- To defend well in our own half and limit the space and time our opponents have to make decisions, with the basic aim of winning the ball.

- To quickly pass the ball forward after winning it and neutralise the immediate pressure from the opposition.

- To play through the lines so that many opposition players are left behind the ball.

- To move the ball into space quickly and effectively to the right players in attacking positions.

- When the transition from defence to attack takes place in the low zone, there is often a lot of space in the opponent's half to exploit - this means the team can get quickly in behind the defensive line to create scoring opportunities.

- Support our forwards with players making fast runs from deep positions.

- Play the ball into the spaces so that we can implement a fast break attack. Take advantage of the space and our speed of movement against the opposing defenders.

- Counter attacks from the low zone (from the time we win the ball to the finish) take 8-12 seconds on average.

What Practices/Sessions Can We Create for this Tactical Situation?

- We must practice our defensive organisation and cohesive movements in our own half against an organised attack. We aim to block the channels to our goal and win the ball.

- Once the ball is won, we need to work on passing the ball quickly forward into the spaces where we can be most effective.

- We work on fast and effective transitions from defence to attack - practicing various tactical situations with equality of numbers or with a numerical advantage (overload situations).

TACTICAL SITUATION 1

PEP GUARDIOLA TACTICS

Exploiting Free Space in the Opposition Half with a Fast Counter Attack

Content taken from Analysis of Bayern Munich during the 2013/2014 Bundesliga winning season

The analysis is based on recurring patterns of play observed within the Bayern Munich team. Once the same phase of play occurred a number of times (at least 10) the tactics would be seen as a pattern. The analysis on the next page is an example of the team's tactics being used effectively, taken from a specific game.

Each action, pass, individual movement with or without the ball, and the positioning of each player on the pitch including their body shape, are presented.

The analysis is then used to create a full progressive session to coach this specific tactical situation.

Exploiting Space in the Opposition Half with a Fast Counter Attack

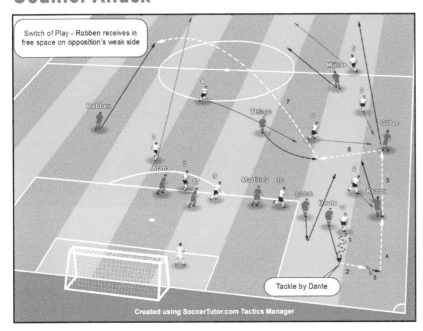

Switch of Play - Robben receives in free space on opposition's weak side

Tackle by Dante

Created using SoccerTutor.com Tactics Manager

In this example, Borussia Dortmund are attacking down Bayern's right side. All of the outfield players are in one half. If Bayern are able to win the ball, they have an opportunity to exploit the space in the opposition's half.

The centre back (Dante) is able to dispossess the left winger Reus (11) and then pass up the line to Kroos, who passes forward to Götze. Thiago drops back to receive the next pass and switches play into the space on the left where Robben has made a forward run.

Created using SoccerTutor.com Tactics Manager

As Robben runs forward with the ball, Müller and Götze make fast supporting runs.

Robben is too quick for his marker and arrives in the box unchallenged. He could have passed to Müller or Götze to finish, but on this occasion he used a clever chip finish to score the goal.

Bayern were able to fully exploit the space in the opposition half with quick combination play and an excellent long pass to switch the play.

45

SESSION FOR THIS TACTICAL SITUATION (4 PRACTICES)
1.Transition Play in a 2 Zone Possession Game

Yellows aim to complete 5/6 passes or keep ball for 30 secs = 1 point

If reds win the ball and pass to opposite side = 1 point

Created using SoccerTutor.com Tactics Manager

Objective: To develop fast transitions from defence to attack and attacking space in the opposition's half.

Description

In a 20 x 25 yard area, we divide the pitch into 2 equal grids. We have 2 teams of 4 players (red & yellow) and 2 neutral players (blue) positioned on the end line of each zone, who play with the team in possession.

The practice starts in one grid with one team in possession (yellows in example) and the objective is to complete 5-6 passes or keep the ball for 30 seconds (1 point) with the help of 2 blue neutral players.

The defending team (reds) must press and try to win the ball. If they are successful, they must then quickly switch the play to a neutral player positioned on the end line in the opposite grid (1 point). The reds then move across with the objective to maintain possession with the blue neutral players, and the yellows become the defenders.

Rules: Players have unlimited touches (or 2-3 touches) but the neutral players are limited to 1-2 touches.

Coaching Points

1. The defenders must try to reduce the space for their opponents and apply as much collective pressure as possible to win the ball.
2. In the transition from defence to attack, there needs to be good awareness, quick decision making, high tempo actions, fast support play and movement.

PROGRESSION

2. Transition Play in a Directional 2 Zone Possession Game with Set Formations

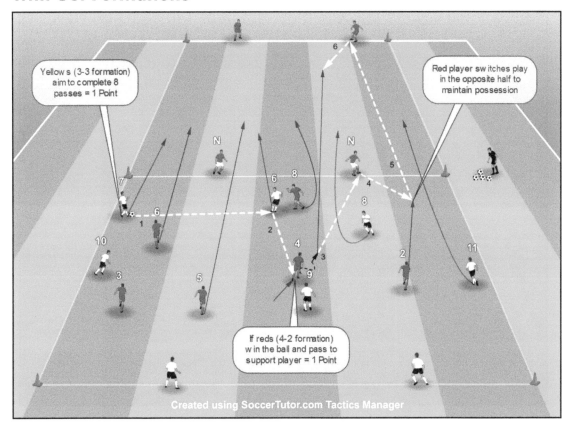

Yellows (3-3 formation) aim to complete 8 passes = 1 Point

Red player switches play in the opposite half to maintain possession

If reds (4-2 formation) win the ball and pass to support player = 1 Point

Created using SoccerTutor.com Tactics Manager

Description

In a 20 x 40 yard area, we divide the pitch into 2 equal grids. We have 2 teams of 8 players (reds & yellows) and 2 neutral players (blues) who remain positioned on the middle line and play with the team in possession. Out of their 8 players, each team has 2 support players positioned on the end lines, as shown in the diagram.

One team (reds) use a 4-2 formation and the other team (yellows) use a 3-3 formation. In this progression, we have the exact same objectives and functionality as the previous practice, but we now play a directional game in set formations. Each team has the support of their outside players in their half.

Rules

1. If a team completes 8 consecutive passes = 1 point.
2. If a team manages to pass to a support player and a neutral player within the same sequence = 2 points.
3. Players have unlimited touches (or 2-3 touches) but the neutral players are limited to 1-2 touches.
4. When a team is in transition from defence to attack, all of the players on that team should move across to the other grid within 5 seconds.

PROGRESSION

3. Exploiting Space in the Opposition Half with a Fast Counter Attack in a SSG with Support Players

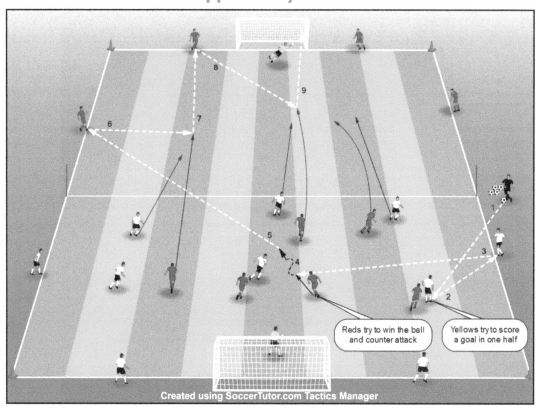

Reds try to win the ball and counter attack

Yellows try to score a goal in one half

Created using SoccerTutor.com Tactics Manager

Description

In a 40 x 50 yard area, we divide the pitch into 2 equal grids. Each team has 6 outfield players and 4 outside support players in the positions shown. We also have 2 full size goals with goalkeepers.

One team (yellows in example) start the practice attacking in the opponent's half and try to score a goal (1 point). The other team (reds) defend in this half and try to win the ball before launching a fast counter attack with the help of their outside support players. If a team scores with a counter attack they get 2 points. When the attack is finished, the practice starts in the other half and the 2 teams switch roles.

Rules: The team in the possession phase have unlimited touches (outside support players have 1-2 touches). The counter attacking team are limited to 2-3 touches and have a set amount of time to finish their attack.

Coaching Points

1. Use ball oriented defence and press as a unit to limit space/time and apply as much pressure as possible.
2. After winning the ball, the players need to react very quickly to the situation (transition from defence to attack) and demonstrate good decision making, movement and intelligence in their runs.
3. Counter attack at a high tempo, with good awareness, fast support and movement, quick decision making, accurate combination play, good communication and one touch finishing.

PROGRESSION

4. Exploiting Space in the Opposition Half with a Fast Counter Attack in an 11 v 11 Two Zone Game

Yellows try to score a goal in one half

Reds try to win the ball and counter attack by first playing through the wide blue gates

Created using SoccerTutor.com Tactics Manager

Description

In the final practice of this session we use a full pitch and play 11 v 11. We again divide the pitch into 2 equal halves, as shown in the diagram. The red team are in a 4-2-3-1 (or 4-4-1-1) formation and the yellow team are in a 4-3-3 formation. You can adjust the formations to suit your team's training.

The practice starts with the yellow No.6 in the centre circle. All of the players start in this half except for 1 red forward, 2 yellow centre backs and the yellow team's goalkeeper (the 2 red wingers are positioned in the blue cone gates). The yellows try to penetrate the red's organised defensive line and score a goal (1 point).

The objective for the red team is to play with good ball oriented defence in the low zone, win the ball and then quickly pass out wide (through the blue cone gates) and into the space to counter attack. If the reds score within 10-12 seconds of winning the ball, the goal counts double. Change team roles after 10 minutes.

Rules

1. The 2 red wingers (7 & 11) and the No.10 are the only players allowed to join the counter attack -> 4 v 3.
2. No.6 is the only yellow player allowed to track back into his own half.

TACTICAL SITUATION 2

DIEGO SIMEONE TACTICS

Press, Win the Ball + Counter Attack with Quick Combination Play in Limited Space

Content taken from Analysis of Atlético Madrid during the 2013/2014 La Liga winning season

The analysis is based on recurring patterns of play observed within the Atlético Madrid team. Once the same phase of play occurred a number of times (at least 10) the tactics would be seen as a pattern. The analysis on the next page is an example of the team's tactics being used effectively, taken from a specific game.

Each action, pass, individual movement with or without the ball, and the positioning of each player on the pitch including their body shape, are presented.

The analysis is then used to create a full progressive session to coach this specific tactical situation.

Analysis Taken from 'Atlético Madrid vs Barcelona - 21 Aug 2013' (Supercopa de España)'

Press, Win the Ball + Counter Attack with Quick Combination Play in Limited Space

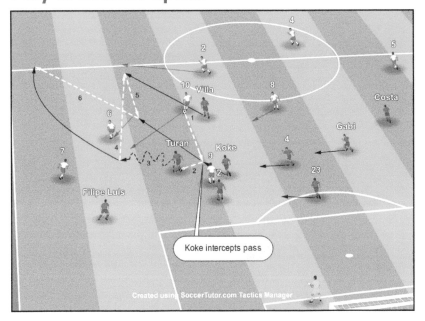

Koke intercepts pass

Atlético Madrid are defending in the low zone in a compact formation with many players in the centre. The Atlético striker (Villa) closes down the ball carrier No.10 who tries to pass to the striker (9). No.9 is surrounded by 3 Atlético players and the central midfielder Koke is able to intercept the pass.

Koke passes to Turan who runs forward with the ball and passes to Villa. Villa passes back to Koke who has made a forward run, and he passes to Turan who has made a run into the space on the left.

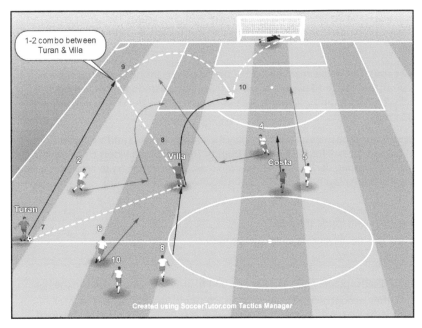

1-2 combo between Turan & Villa

Turan is able to pass to Villa in space in the centre as he has made a forward run.

Turan makes a long fast run up the flank to receive the return pass.

Villa continues running forwards and volleys the cross first time into the far corner.

This quick counter attack was possible due to the initial quick combination play and the supporting runs of both Turan and Villa.

SESSION FOR THIS TACTICAL SITUATION (3 PRACTICES)
1. Press, Win the Ball and Support Play in an 8 v 4 (+6) Possession Game

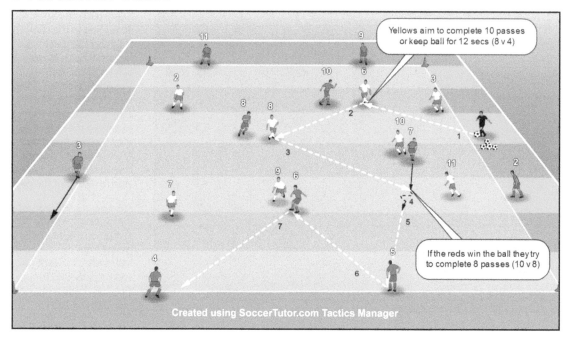

Yellows aim to complete 10 passes or keep ball for 12 secs (8 v 4)

If the reds win the ball they try to complete 8 passes (10 v 8)

Created using SoccerTutor.com Tactics Manager

Objective: The players work on keeping possession after the transition from defence to attack.

Description

In a 35 x 35 yard area, we have 2 teams. The yellow team have all of their 8 players inside the area, using a 2-3-3 formation (from 4-3-3). The red team have 10 players in a 4-4-2 formation (diamond midfield used in diagram example). 2 centre backs, 2 full backs and 2 forwards are positioned outside the area in the positions shown and the 4 midfielders are inside.

The practice starts with the yellow team in possession and they play 8 v 4 inside the area and aim to complete 10 consecutive passes (1 point) or keep the ball for 12 seconds (2 points). The 4 red midfielders try to win the ball or force their opponents into making a wrong decision. If the reds win the ball, they then try to keep possession against the yellow team, using the outside players to support (8 consecutive passes = 1 point).

Rules

1. The red outside players are not allowed inside the area.
2. The yellow players and the red outside players are limited to 2 touches.

Coaching Points

1. The red midfielders (numerical disadvantage) need to press as a unit to limit space/time and win the ball.
2. After the reds recover the ball, they need to exhibit the following attributes: Speed, power, quality of pass, good decision making, one-touch passing, correct angles and distances for support play and good communication to avoid pressure from their opponents.

PROGRESSION

2. Press, Win the Ball and Support Play in a Dynamic 3 Zone Possession Game

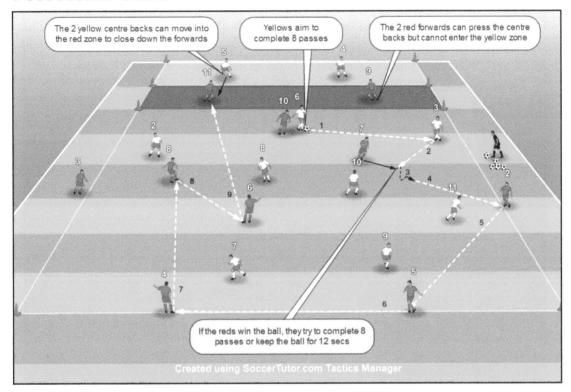

The 2 yellow centre backs can move into the red zone to close down the forwards

Yellows aim to complete 8 passes

The 2 red forwards can press the centre backs but cannot enter the yellow zone

If the reds win the ball, they try to complete 8 passes or keep the ball for 12 secs

Created using SoccerTutor.com Tactics Manager

Description

This is a progression of the previous practice and we have the exact same objective and point scoring system. We increase the area slightly to 35 yards x 40 yards and mark out 2 extra zones at one end (2.5 yards each).

In the red zone there are 2 red forwards (11 & 9) and in the yellow zone there are 2 yellow centre backs (4 & 5). Both teams have 10 players each using the 4-4-2 formation. You can adapt the practice to play with whatever formation you want.

As with the previous practice, we start with the yellow team in possession. If the reds win the ball, they then try to keep possession against the yellow team, using the outside players to support.

Rules

1. When the yellow team are in possession and the ball is played into the yellow centre back zone, the 2 red forwards can press the centre backs, but must stay within their zone. Their aim is to block/intercept passes.

2. When the reds are in possession, the 2 yellow centre backs are allowed to enter the red forwards' zone and apply pressure to try and win the ball.

3. If the yellow team complete 8 consecutive passes they score 1 point.

4. If the red team complete 8 consecutive passes they score 1 point and if they keep possession for 12 seconds, they score 2 points.

PROGRESSION

3. Press, Win the Ball + Counter Attack with Quick Combination Play in Limited Space (Zonal Game)

Yellow players can only track back once the ball has passed the halfway line

Yellow team start position with the aim to score a goal

Red team try to win ball and score with a counter attack within 10-12 secs

Created using SoccerTutor.com Tactics Manager

Description

In this progression of the previous practice, we mark out 3 zones on a full pitch (as shown in the diagram) and we add 2 full size goals with goalkeepers.

The practice starts with a yellow centre back (4 or 5) and the yellow team's aim is to score a goal. The red team must defend well in the low zone, try to win the ball and then make a quick transition from defence to attack (under pressure from the yellows). A minimum of 2 red players should leave the large zone to support the 2 forwards (9 & 11) and launch a fast break attack, finishing within 10-12 seconds.

Rules

1. The 8 yellow players in the large zone can only track back once the ball has crossed the halfway line.
2. The 2 yellow centre backs are allowed to enter the forwards' zone and apply pressure to try and win the ball.
3. A yellow goal scores 1 point and a red goal scores 2 points (as long as it is completed within 10-12 seconds).

Coaching Points

1. The red players need to press as a unit to limit space/time in the first phase to win the ball.
2. There needs to be a rhythm to the timing of movement/runs, combined with good communication.
3. Players need to use quality and effective finishing in front of goal - using 1 touch whenever possible.

TACTICAL SITUATION 3

CLAUDIO RANIERI TACTICS

Defensive Organisation to Win the Ball and Fast Running to Counter Attack

Content taken from Analysis of Leicester City FC during the 2015/2016 Premier League winning season

The analysis is based on recurring patterns of play observed within the Leicester City team. Once the same phase of play occurred a number of times (at least 10) the tactics would be seen as a pattern. The analysis on the next page is an example of the team's tactics being used effectively, taken from a specific game.

Each action, pass, individual movement with or without the ball, and the positioning of each player on the pitch including their body shape, are presented.

The analysis is then used to create a full progressive session to coach this specific tactical situation.

Analysis Taken from 'Norwich City vs Leicester City FC - 3 Oct 2015'

Defensive Organisation to Win the Ball and Fast Running to Support Counter Attack

> Schlupp tackles No.2 and runs forward with the ball

In this example, the opposition are attacking and Leicester are organised well defensively.

Okazaki puts the ball carrier under pressure, which enables Schlupp to win the ball. He immediately runs forward with the ball.

The central midfielder (Kante), the winger (Albrighton) and the striker (Vardy) all make forward runs to support the fast break attack.

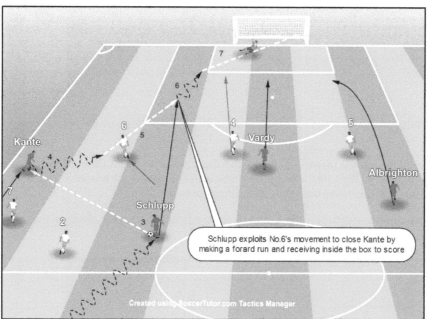

> Schlupp exploits No.6's movement to close Kante by making a forard run and receiving inside the box to score

Schlupp passes to Kante who is free in space on the left side. As he is closed down by an opponent, Kante is able to play a pass into the box for Schlupp who has continued his run forward (support play - pass and move).

Schlupp had the option to pass to Vardy or Albrighton who made fast supporting runs, but is able to finish himself into the far corner.

1. Defending in a 4 v 4 Situation and Quick Transition to 4 v 2 Counter Attack

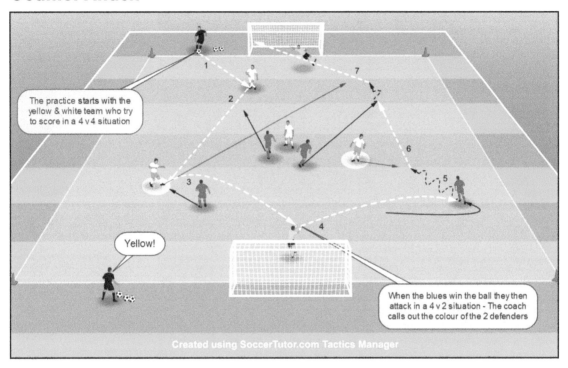

The practice starts with the yellow & white team who try to score in a 4 v 4 situation

Yellow!

When the blues win the ball they then attack in a 4 v 2 situation - The coach calls out the colour of the 2 defenders

Created using SoccerTutor.com Tactics Manager

Objective: To develop fast transitions from defence to attack.

Description

In a 25 x 25 yard area we have a full size goal with a goalkeeper at both ends as shown. We have one team (blue) with 4 players and another team of 4 with 2 yellow players and 2 white players who play together. The practice starts with the yellow and white team who try to score past the blue team's goalkeeper (4 v 4 situation).

The objective for the blue team is to first defend and win the ball. If they are successful, they then make a very quick transition from defence to attack against 2 players (4 v 2 situation). The coach calls out either 'Yellow' or 'White' as soon as the blues win the ball - this determines which 2 players defend the attack. The other 2 players (whites in diagram example) stand still and do not take part in the rest of the phase.

If the ball goes out of play when the blues are defending or their yellow and white opponents score, the same transition happens with the coach passing in a new ball, calling out 'Yellow' or 'White' to determine which 2 players defend the attack.

Rules

1. All players have unlimited touches.
2. The transition to attack (4 v 2) must be finished within 8-10 seconds.

Coaching Point: Play the ball into spaces so that we attack quickly. Take advantage of the space and speed of movement against the defenders.

PROGRESSION

2. Counter Attacks in a Dynamic 3 Zone Transition Game

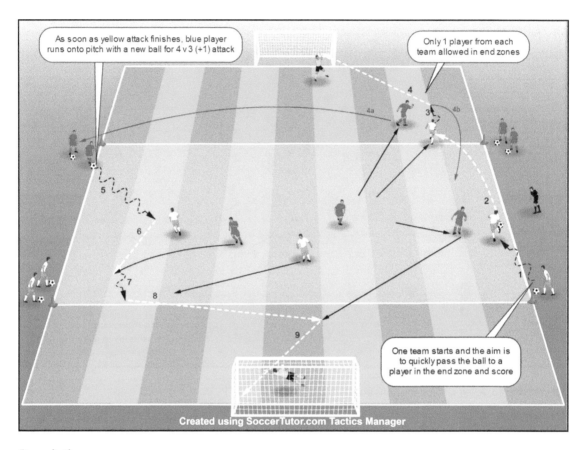

As soon as yellow attack finishes, blue player runs onto pitch with a new ball for 4 v 3 (+1) attack

Only 1 player from each team allowed in end zones

One team starts and the aim is to quickly pass the ball to a player in the end zone and score

Created using SoccerTutor.com Tactics Manager

Description

In a 30 x 40 yard area we divide the pitch into 3 zones. The 2 end zones are 30 x 10 yards and the middle zone is 30 x 20 yards. Each team has 4 inside players and a goalkeeper defending a full size goal.

One team starts with the ball (yellows in diagram) and the aim is to quickly pass the ball to a player in the end zone and score. When the yellow's attack is finished, one of the defending team's outside players (blues in diagram) dribbles a ball onto the pitch and starts a new attack in the opposite direction (the blue defender in the end zone moves to the outside). His team (blues) must move quickly from defence to attack in a 4 v 3 (+1) situation (the yellow player who finished the last attack tracks back as the +1).

The practice should be continuous and uninterrupted at a high tempo. The players rest when they are outside.

Rules

1. Only 1 player from each team is allowed in an end zone at any time.
2. Free time and unlimited touches for all players / Limit the time for finishing the attacks to 10 seconds and limit the players to 2-3 touches in the end zones.

3. Defensive Organisation to Win the Ball and Fast Running to Support Counter Attacks in a Zonal Practice

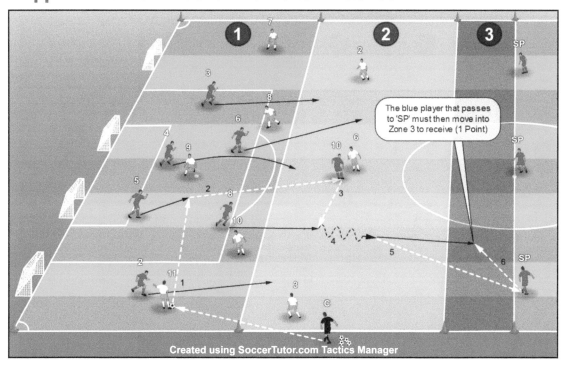

The blue player that passes to 'SP' must then move into Zone 3 to receive (1 Point)

Created using SoccerTutor.com Tactics Manager

Description

Using half a full pitch, we mark out 3 zones and have 4 mini goals on the end line, as shown in the diagram. The blue team have 7 players in a 4-2-1 formation (from 4-2-3-1, 4-4-1-1 or 4-3-3) and 3 support players on the halfway line. The yellow team have 8 players in a 2-3-3 formation with 2 full backs (from 4-3-3).

The practice starts with the yellows in zone 1 trying to score in one of the 4 mini goals (1 point). The blue team defend the 4 mini goals, try to win the ball and then pass quickly to one of the support players, either by first passing into zone 2 or directly.

The player that passes the ball to a support player must then quickly run into the 'Passer Zone' (3) to receive a pass back, which scores 1 point. This replicates passing to a forward and then quickly supporting them for an attack. While this is happening, the whole blue team must move quickly from zone 1 into zone 2 (whilst retaining team shape), pushing the entire team forward. This must be done before the pass is received back in the 'Passer Zone'.

Coaching Points

1. The defending team (blues) use ball oriented defence and press as a unit to limit time and space - applying as much pressure as possible to win the ball. The defenders need to maintain the correct distances between each other and have good communication when applying pressure.

2. In the transition from defence to attack, there needs to be good awareness and quick support play (running). All movements should be done at a high tempo.

PROGRESSION

4. Defensive Organisation to Win the Ball and Fast Running to Support Counter Attacks in a Dynamic 4 Zone Game

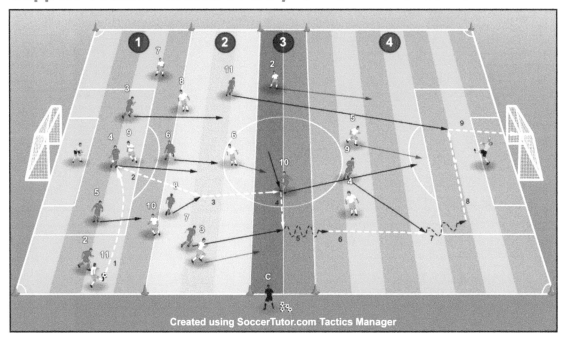

Created using SoccerTutor.com Tactics Manager

Description

In this final practice, we use a full pitch and mark out a 10 yard zone in the centre as shown. The blue team are in a 4-4-2 (or 4-4-1-1) formation and the yellows are in a 4-3-3 formation. The practice starts with the yellows attacking the blue team and trying to score. The blues defend with 8 outfield players but they have 1 forward in the opposition half (9) and another forward (10) in the 'Passer Zone' (zone 3).

The aim for the blue team is to win the ball and pass to No.10 in the 'Passer Zone' - any player can then move forward to receive the ball back within zone 3 and launch a fast break attack. The blue players should look to play forward and use the space in the opponent's half to exploit the defensive imbalance of the yellow team.

Once the ball is played out from zone 1, the blue players must quickly move forward into zone 2, pushing the entire team forward. This must be done before the pass is received back in the 'Passer Zone'.

The attack should take a maximum of 15 seconds from winning the ball - if not, the practice starts again with the yellow team's goalkeeper and the blues take up their starting positions. The blue team's goals count double.

Coaching Points

1. The blue team use ball oriented defence and press as a unit to limit time/space when applying pressure.
2. In the transition from defence to attack, there needs to be good awareness, decision making, quick support and cohesive forward movements. There also needs to be combination play at a high tempo, individuality, aggression and quick and effective finishing.

60

TACTICAL SITUATION 4

PEP GUARDIOLA TACTICS

Fast Transition to Attack from the Back: Exploiting Space in Behind

Content taken from Analysis of Bayern Munich during the 2013/2014 Bundesliga winning season

The analysis is based on recurring patterns of play observed within the Bayern Munich team. Once the same phase of play occurred a number of times (at least 10) the tactics would be seen as a pattern. The analysis on the next page is an example of the team's tactics being used effectively, taken from a specific game.

Each action, pass, individual movement with or without the ball, and the positioning of each player on the pitch including their body shape, are presented.

The analysis is then used to create a full progressive session to coach this specific tactical situation.

Fast Transition to Attack from the Back: Exploiting Space in Behind

Vidal (23) intercepts the ball and passes to Costa, who makes a clever touch to Rafinha who runs forward with the ball

In this example, the opposition have played a short corner and the ball ends up with the left back (3) who tries to play a ball into the box, but miss-hits it straight to Vidal (23).

Vidal (23) clears and Costa is able to get to the ball before the left back and makes a clever touch (pass) to the right back Rafinha.

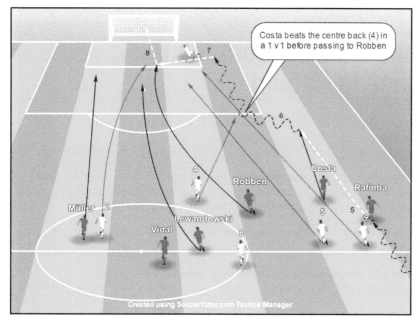

Costa beats the centre back (4) in a 1 v 1 before passing to Robben

Rafinha runs with the ball into the opposition half and plays the ball into Costa's path.

Costa carries the ball to the edge of the box, beats the centre back (5) in a 1 v 1 and then runs towards the byline.

The goalkeeper comes out of goal, so Costa cuts the ball back to Robben who has made a long supporting run to finish.

Bayern had 5 players in total making runs into the box to provide support for this successful counter attack.

SESSION FOR THIS TACTICAL SITUATION (3 PRACTICES)
1. Transition and Support Play in a Dynamic 3 Zone Game

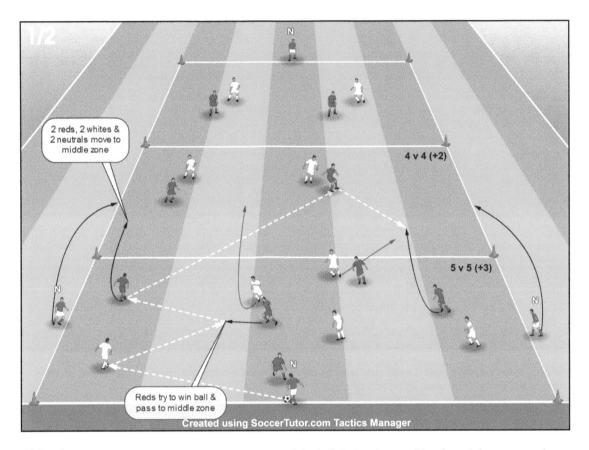

Objective: To develop the ability to keep possession of the ball during the transition from defence to attack.

Description

In a 30 x 54 yard area we mark out 3 equal zones (30 x 18 yards each). In the low zone we have 5 reds against 5 white players. We also have 3 blue neutral outside players which creates a 5 v 5 (+3) situation.

In the middle zone we start with 2 players from each team. In the high zone we also have 2 players from each team and a blue neutral player at the end.

The practice starts with one team in possession in the low zone (whites in example). The aim is to complete 5-6 consecutive passes with the help of the 3 neutral players and then pass the ball into the middle zone.

The aim for the defending team (reds) is to press collectively, win the ball and pass quickly into the middle zone. This is demonstrated in the diagram example.

When a team passes the ball into the middle zone, the following players move from the low zone to create a 4 v 4 (+2) situation: 2 red players, 2 white players and the 2 blue neutral players at the sides.

63

3 v 3 (+1)

Aim = Complete 5-6 passes & pass to high zone

4 v 4 (+2)

Created using SoccerTutor.com Tactics Manager

As 2 red players, 2 white players and 2 neutral players have moved from the low zone into the middle zone we now have a 4 v 4 (+2) situation in the middle zone.

Once either team plays the ball into the middle zone, the aim is to complete 5-6 consecutive passes with the help of the 2 neutral players and then pass the ball into the high zone.

When a team passes the ball into the high zone, 1 red player and 1 white player move into the high zone from the middle zone. There is 1 neutral player on the end line which creates a 3 v 3 (+1) situation.

The aim for the red team is to complete 5-6 passes and transfer the ball back to the middle zone. If they are successful, they then aim to pass the ball into the low zone with the respective players' movements. The whites aim to win the ball and then do the same. The practice is continuous.

Coaching Points

1. Players should look to use a maximum of 2 touches (control and pass), so the ball is moved quickly and the opposition are not able to close down the ball carrier and dispossess him.
2. Support teammates in the next zone by making fast runs forward to receive a one touch pass back. This then makes it much easier for the team to maintain possession and progress through the zones.

PROGRESSION

2. Fast Transition to Attack from the Back by Exploiting Space in Behind in a 3 Zone SSG

Reds aim to win ball in zone 1 and then counter attack via the support players (SP) in zones 2 & 3

Created using SoccerTutor.com Tactics Manager

Description

In a 30 x 45 yard area we divide the pitch into 3 equal zones (30 x 15 yards each) and we have 2 full size goals with goalkeepers. Each team has 5 outfield players who start in the low zone. There are also 2 support players (blue) with 1 in the middle zone and 1 in the end zone.

One team starts with the ball in the low zone (whites) and tries to score. The reds defend and try to win the ball before passing to the support player in the middle zone. They then make a quick transition to attack as all their players move into the middle zone. The white players also move into the middle zone to track back and defend.

Once all the red players are in the middle zone, they can pass to the support player in the high zone and finish the attack very quickly. The practice then starts in the low zone again but the team's roles are reversed - the red team attack and the white team try to win the ball and make a quick transition from defence to attack.

Rules

1. The team that starts with the ball (whites in diagram) have unlimited touches and the team that makes the transition from defence to attack are limited to 2/3 touches. The support players are limited to 1/2 touches.
2. Players have 5 seconds to move into next zone, or the game is stopped and the ball given to the opposition.

PROGRESSION

3. Fast Transition to Attack from the Back by Exploiting Space in Behind the Opponent's Defensive Line

GK starts practice against 2 red forwards in their own half

The reds aim to keep compact in their half, win the ball and then counter attack quickly

Created using SoccerTutor.com Tactics Manager

Description

For the final practice in this session we use a full pitch divided into 2 halves. The reds are in a 4-4-2 formation and the whites are in a 4-3-3 formation. The practice starts with the white team's goalkeeper.

To start we have a 4 v 2 situation in one half as the whites aim to pass into their attacking half. Once the ball is played into the other half, there are no longer any restrictions of movement across the 2 halves. The aim for the reds is to draw their opponents deep into the low zone and win the ball - they then make a quick transition from defence to attack in the open pitch, exploiting the free space in behind the defensive line of their opponents.

Rules

1. The red team's counter attack must be finished within 15 seconds. If not, the practice starts again with the white team's goalkeeper and the red players take up their start positions.
2. A goal for the red team counts double.

Coaching Points

1. The red team use ball oriented defence and press as a unit to limit the time/space available.
2. In the transition to attack, there needs to be good awareness, decision making, quick support play, fast running, quick combination play, individual 1 v 1 play, aggression and effective finishing.

CHAPTER 5

TRANSITION FROM DEFENCE TO ATTACK IN THE MIDDLE ZONE

TRANSITION FROM DEFENCE TO ATTACK IN THE MIDDLE ZONE

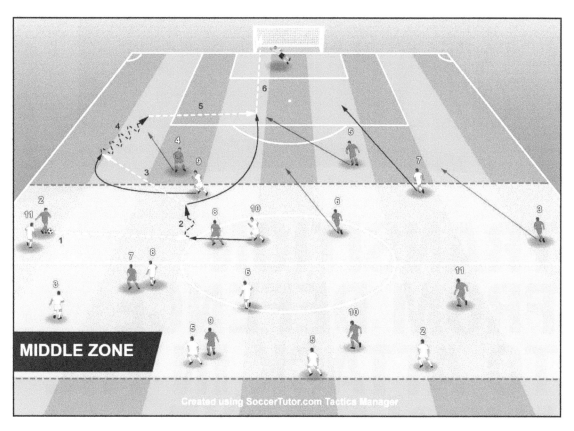

MIDDLE ZONE

For this book, we have divided the chapters by which zone the transition starts in. There are 3 zones:

1. **Low Zone**

2. Middle Zone

3. **High Zone**

This diagram shows an example of a team that has won the ball in the middle zone. In this situation, the white team have players behind the ball when defending. To win the ball, they need to limit their opponent's time/space, block potential passing options and demonstrate good anticipation.

The red team are trying to build up play from the back. The right back (2) had received a pass from the centre back and is closed down by the white team's left

winger (11). The attempted pass inside to red No.8 is intercepted by the white No.10.

The No.10 runs forward with the ball and the red team are left unbalanced. The striker (9) makes a run out wide and receives the pass. The red centre back (4) has to follow him, which creates space in the centre for the No.10 to run into. No.9 dribbles towards the box and passes the ball across to No.10 to finish. The right winger (7) also makes a run into the box to support the attack.

The aim after winning the ball in the middle zone should always be to pass/move the ball forward quickly to exploit the disorganised defence of the opposition, before they have time to recover.

What is the Tactical Situation?

- Our team defends higher up the pitch and further from our goal, compared to when we defend in the low zone.

- There are many players from both teams in the centre of the pitch.

- We are now closer to the opponent's goal when we win the ball.

- We have the option of many attacking solutions when we win the ball.

- We can attack with up to 5 or 6 players.

- 2-3 players can more easily run beyond the forwards to offer options.

- Quick attacks from the middle zone have a higher chance of success than the low zone. The opposition are often unorganised when they lose the ball in this area.

- There is often free space behind the opponent's defensive line to exploit.

- There are possibilities to create a numerical advantage (overload situation).

- The attacks (transition from defence to attack) take 8 seconds on average.

What Objectives Should We Have?

- To defend well in our own half, limiting the time and space our opponents have while pressing to win the ball.

- To quickly pass the ball forward and exploit the unorganised defence of our opponents.

- Quick combination play - one-touch passing and passes into space.

- To run forward with the ball at speed, drawing opponents in and beating them or creating space for teammates to run into before passing to them.

- To quickly run up from behind, to support our striker, ask for the ball to be played into the space and finish the attacks.

- Quick, quality and synchronised movements inside the penalty area to finish the attacks effectively.

What Practices/Sessions Can We Create for this Tactical Situation?

- Work on defensive situations in the middle zone versus opponents trying to attack in behind the defensive line, with the primary aim to win the ball.

- The players need to learn how to move and pass the ball quickly forward to players in advanced positions, so that we can attack quickly while the opposition are still unbalanced.

- The main focus of the practices needs to be on fast and effective transitions from defence to attack with equal numbers or with a numerical advantage (overload situations).

TACTICAL SITUATION 1

JÜRGEN KLOPP TACTICS

Fast Break Attack from the Middle Zone

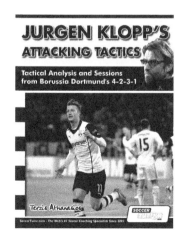

Analysis taken from 'Jürgen Klopp's Attacking Tactics' (Athanasios Terzis 2015)

Available to buy from SoccerTutor.com (paperback + eBook)

The analysis is based on recurring patterns of play. Once the same phase of play occurred a number of times (at least 10) the tactics would be decoded, with the positioning of each player on the pitch studied in great detail, including their body shape. Each individual movement with or without the ball was also recorded in detail. The analysis on the next page is an example of the team's tactics being used effectively.

The analysis is then used to create a full progressive session to coach this specific tactical situation.

Analysis taken from 'Jürgen Klopp's Attacking Tactics' (Athanasios Terzis)

Fast Break Attack from the Middle Zone

After 2 consecutive passes by the opposition, the ball is played towards the central midfielder (8).

Mkhitaryan (10) moves across to contest him and intercepts the pass.

Mkhitaryan (10) moves forward with the ball. Lewandowski (9) moves towards the available space on the left and receives the pass on the run, while Reus (11) moves towards the centre. Aubameyang (17) moves between the 2 centre backs who converge to secure the central zone.

Lewandowski (9) dribbles inside and can play the ball into the penalty area for Aubameyang (17) or pass back to Reus (11).

SESSION FOR THIS TACTICAL SITUATION (5 PRACTICES)
1. Transition Play in a 4 (+3) v 4 Possession Game

Aim: Win the ball, pass & then all 4 players move (swap) to outside positions

Objective: To develop the ability to keep possession of the ball during the transition from defence to attack.

Description

In an 8 x 16 yard area, we have 2 teams of 4 players and 3 neutrals players (blue). One team (yellow) starts inside the area with 1 neutral player. The other 2 neutral players move along the 2 end lines. The other team (reds) have their players on the outsides as shown in the diagram.

The reds and the neutral players aim to keep possession. The objective for the defenders (yellows in the diagram) is to win the ball and pass to one of the 3 neutral players. At this point they quickly run to the outside, switching positions with the red team. Now the yellows and neutrals are in possession and the red team are the defenders The practice continues with the roles reversed and is continuous.

Rules

1. The outside players and the neutrals are limited to 2 touches / The outside players and the neutrals on the end lines are limited to 2 touches and the inside neutral player has 1 touch.

2. If the outside players and neutral players complete 8 consecutive passes they score 1 point.

PROGRESSION
2. Fast Break Attacks in a Dynamic Transition Game

Yellow Aim: Win the ball + attack
either goal within 8 seconds

Red & Blue Aim:
8-10 Consecutive Passes

Created using SoccerTutor.com Tactics Manager

Objective: To work on quick counter attacks after winning the ball - when the opposition are still unorganised.

Description

In a 20 x 50 yard area, we divide the pitch into 3 zones. The central zone is 20 x 26 yards and the 2 end zones are 20 x 12 yards. We have a full size goal at both ends with goalkeepers. The situation and player positions in the central zone are exactly the same as the previous practice - refer back if you need to.

The difference in this practice is that when the defending team (yellows) win the ball, their objective now is to try and score in either of the 2 goals as quickly as possible.

Rules

1. 2 neutral players and 2 red outside players can defend the attack, but they are not allowed to enter the end zone until the ball has been played in there.

2. The players in the transition from defence to attack (yellows in diagram example) have unlimited touches, but they have a limited time to finish their attack (e.g. 8 seconds).

PROGRESSION

3. Fast Break Attacks in a Position Specific Transition Game (1)

Objective: To work on fast break attacks after winning the ball when the opposition are still unorganised.

Description

In a 45 x 60 yard area we divide the pitch into 3 zones. The central zone is 45 x 30 yards and the 2 end zones are 45 x 15 yards each. We position 2 mini goals at each end as shown in the diagram.

We have 2 teams of 6 players in the central zone with 1 neutral player inside and 2 positioned wide on the outsides. Each team also has an extra support player (SP) in one end zone.

One team starts in possession (reds in diagram) and tries to score in one of the 2 mini goals with the help of the neutral players. The yellows aim to press, win the ball and then make a quick transition from defence to attack in the opposite direction and score, making sure to use their support player in the end zone.

Rules

1. All players are free to move outside of the middle zone once a pass to a support player is made.
2. All players have unlimited touches but the neutral/support players are limited to 2 touches.
3. All players have unlimited touches in the central zone and 2-3 touches in the end zones.
4. All players are limited to 2-3 touches but the neutral/support players are limited to 1 touch.

74

PROGRESSION

4. Fast Break Attacks in a Position Specific Transition Game (2)

Must pass to support player (A) before scoring

6 v 6 + 3

Created using SoccerTutor.com Tactics Manager

Description

For this progression of the previous practice, we replace the mini goals with 2 full size goals and goalkeepers. We also have 1 attacker (A) and 1 defender (D) for each team in each end zone (replacing the support players), which makes the fast break attacks more competitive and game realistic.

The objectives and rules remain the same.

Coaching Points

1. The defending team need to have maximum concentration to defend well as a unit, limit the time and space the opposition have and press to win the ball.

2. In the transition from defence to attack, the players need to quickly run forward from deep, to support the attacker in the end zone, ask for the ball to be played into the space and finish the attacks.

3. Quick, quality and synchronised movements are needed to finish the attacks effectively.

PROGRESSION

5. Fast Break Attacks from the Middle Zone in an 11 v 11 Game

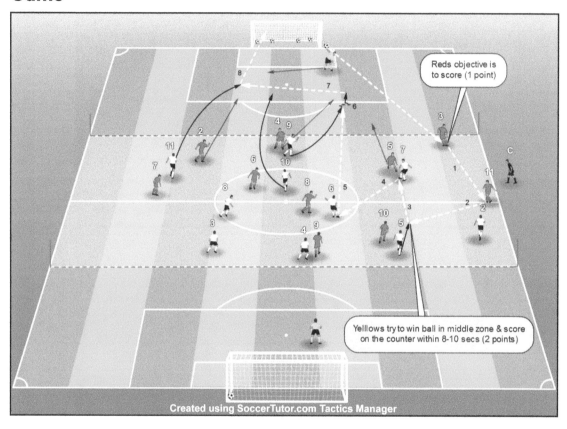

Reds objective is to score (1 point)

Yelllows try to win ball in middle zone & score on the counter within 8-10 secs (2 points)

Created using SoccerTutor.com Tactics Manager

Description

For the final practice in this session, we split the pitch into 3 equal zones. The central zone is the middle defensive zone for the yellow team. The yellow team are in a 4-2-3-1 formation and the red team are in a 4-3-3 formation.

The practice starts with the red team's goalkeeper and the red team in possession as they build up play from the back and try to score (1 point). The middle zone is marked out for the benefit of the yellow team, but the reds do not have any zone restrictions for their attack. If the ball goes out of play, start the practice again with the red team's goalkeeper.

The objective for the yellow team is to apply pressure in the middle zone and win the ball - they then pass the ball forward quickly as they make their transition from defence to attack. If the yellows score they get 1 point. If they score within 8-10 seconds of winning the ball, they get 2 points.

Coaching Points

1. Quick combination play is needed - one-touch passing and passes into space.
2. Look to play passes in between the 2 centre backs or in between the full back and centre back, timed with a good run to receive behind the defensive line.

TACTICAL SITUATION 2

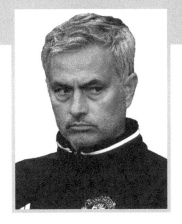

JOSE MOURINHO TACTICS

Creating an Overload with a Fast Break Attack

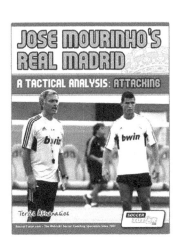

Analysis taken from 'Jose Mourinho's Real Madrid: A Tactical Analysis - Attacking in the 4-2-3-1' (Athanasios Terzis 2012)

Available to buy from SoccerTutor.com (paperback + eBook)

The analysis is based on recurring patterns of play. Once the same phase of play occurred a number of times (at least 10) the tactics would be decoded, with the positioning of each player on the pitch studied in great detail, including their body shape. Each individual movement with or without the ball was also recorded in detail. The analysis on the next page is an example of the team's tactics being used effectively.

The analysis is then used to create a full progressive session to coach this specific tactical situation.

Analysis taken from 'Jose Mourinho's Real Madrid: A Tactical Analysis - Attacking' (Athanasios Terzis)

Creating an Overload with a Fast Break Attack

In this example, Real Madrid's No.10 Ozil wins the ball in midfield.

Ozil moves forward with the ball and Ronaldo moves into a wide position to receive the pass from Ozil on the run.

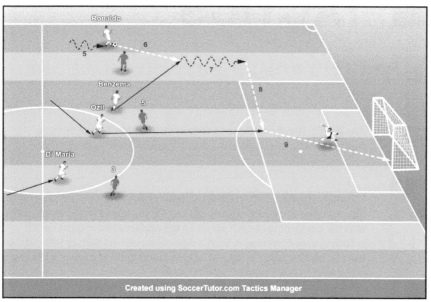

Ronaldo draws one of the centre backs away, so Benzema makes a run in behind him and receives the pass from Ronaldo.

The other centre back (No.5) is drawn to Benzema and the opposition's defenders have large distances between them.

Ozil makes a direct run into the centre forward position. Benzema crosses to him and Ozil scores into the far corner.

COACHING TRANSITION PLAY

SESSION FOR THIS TACTICAL SITUATION (4 PRACTICES)
1. Continuous Fast Attacks with a 5 v 3 Overload

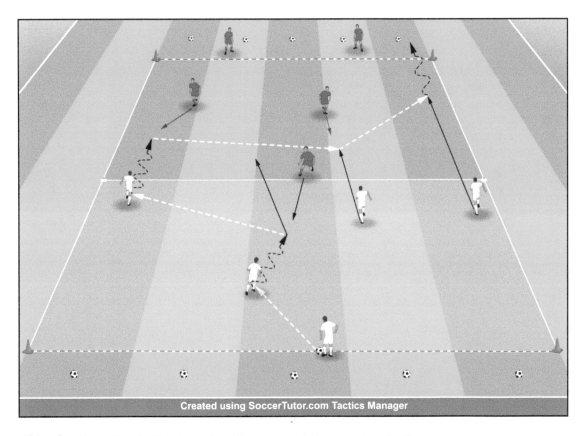

Created using SoccerTutor.com Tactics Manager

Objective: To work on fast break attacks with a numerical advantage (overload).

Description

In a 15 x 25 yard area we have 2 teams of 5 players. Both teams have the objective to score a goal by dribbling the ball across the opponent's goal line. The players start in their own half, but can then move freely after the first pass is played.

One player starts (white in diagram) by passing the ball from his goal line to a teammate and the team then launches a fast attack against 3 defenders (blue). If they carry the ball over the end line, they score 1 point.

Rules

1. All players have unlimited touches.
2. Every attack must be finished within 10 seconds.

When the attack is finished, the ball goes out of play or the defending team win the ball, 2 players from the team which just finished their attack (whites) move to the outside and 3 move back into their half. The other team (blues) then start their 5 v 3 attack with the exact same conditions, in the opposite direction.

79

2. Fast Attacks with a 5 v 3 Overload in a Continuous Small Sided Game

Created using SoccerTutor.com Tactics Manager

Objective: To work on fast break attacks with a numerical advantage (overload).

Description

In a 20 x 40 yard area we split the pitch into 3 zones and use 2 full size goals. The central zone is 20 x 20 yards and both end zones are 20 x 10 yards. Each team has 8-10 outfield players and a goalkeeper.

The practice always starts in the middle zone with one team attacking with a 5 v 3 overload (whites in diagram). All 8 of the outfield players start within the middle zone but can move freely after the first pass. The white team's aim is to utilise their numerical advantage to score a goal within 8-10 seconds.

When the attack is finished, the ball goes out of play or the defending team win the ball, 2 players from the team which just finished their attack (whites) move to the outside.

2 players from the other team (blues) enter the pitch and the blues then start their 5 v 3 attack with the exact same conditions, but in the opposite direction.

PROGRESSION

3. Fast 5 v 3 (+2) Overload Attacks in a Dynamic Transition Game

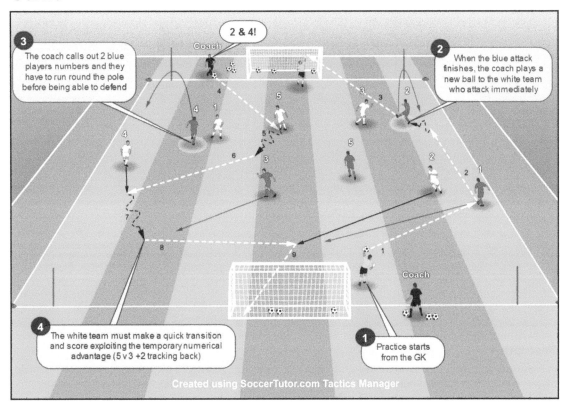

3 The coach calls out 2 blue players numbers and they have to run round the pole before being able to defend

2 & 4! Coach

2 When the blue attack finishes, the coach plays a new ball to the white team who attack immediately

4 The white team must make a quick transition and score exploiting the temporary numerical advantage (5 v 3 +2 tracking back)

1 Practice starts from the GK

Coach

Created using SoccerTutor.com Tactics Manager

Objective: To work on fast break attacks with a numerical advantage (overload).

Description

In a 30 x 30 yard area we have 2 full size goals with goalkeepers. We also have 4 poles positioned near the corners, as shown in the diagram. Both teams have 5 outfield players and they are numbered 1-5.

One team starts with the ball (blues in diagram example) and try to score in the opponent's goal.

When the attack is finished, the ball goes out of play or the defending team win the ball, the 2 players that the coach calls out must run to the corner of the pitch and around a pole before running back inside to join the play. In the diagram example, this is after blue No.2 shoots at goal.

The coach quickly passes a new ball into play and the other team (whites) must make a quick transition from defence to attack and exploit the temporary numerical advantage (5 v 3) they have to score a goal as quickly as possible, before the 2 extra players (No.2 & No.4) are able to track back and help defend.

Coaching Point: The players should sprint towards the poles, then slow down using shorter steps. They can then bend their knees to turn and move off quickly again to sprint back and defend.

4. Fast Break Attacks with Overload in a 3 Zone Transition Game

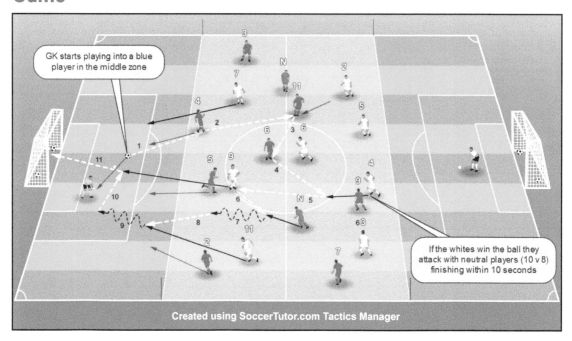

GK starts playing into a blue player in the middle zone

If the whites win the ball they attack with neutral players (10 v 8) finishing within 10 seconds

Created using SoccerTutor.com Tactics Manager

Description

In the final practice of this session we use a full pitch and mark out 3 zones as shown. Both teams have 8 outfield players who all start in the middle zone and are in a 4-1-3 formation. There are also 2 neutral players in the middle zone but they only play with a team that is in transition from defence to attack.

The blue team start in possession in this example and attack in an 8 v 8 situation, trying to score. The players on the defending team (whites) cannot leave the middle zone until the ball has been played beyond it.

The white defending team try to win the ball and make a quick transition from defence to attack. They play with the neutral players (10 v 8 numerical advantage) and try to score with a fast break attack. When the transition is finished, the practice starts with the goalkeeper of the team that just finished their attack.

Different Rules

1. All players have unlimited touches but the neutral players are limited to 3 touches.
2. All players are limited to 3 touches and the neutral players have 2 touches.
3. The transition from defence to attack must be finished within 10 seconds.

Variations

1. You can extend the middle zone to the distance between the 2 penalty areas. This may create a better rhythm for continuous transitions from defence to attack.
2. The neutral players are allowed to act as support players in the first attacking phase, but cannot participate in the finishing of an attack. They still participate fully with the team in transition from defence to attack.

TACTICAL SITUATION 3

DIEGO SIMEONE TACTICS

Fast Break Attacks with Support Players

Content taken from Analysis of Atlético Madrid during the 2014/2015 La Liga winning season

The analysis is based on recurring patterns of play observed within the Atlético Madrid team. Once the same phase of play occurred a number of times (at least 10) the tactics would be seen as a pattern. The analysis on the next page is an example of the team's tactics being used effectively, taken from a specific game.

Each action, pass, individual movement with or without the ball, and the positioning of each player on the pitch including their body shape, are presented.

The analysis is then used to create a full progressive session to coach this specific tactical situation.

Analysis Taken from 'Atlético Madrid vs Real Madrid - 15 Jan 2015 (Copa Del Ray)'
Fast Break Attacks with Support Players

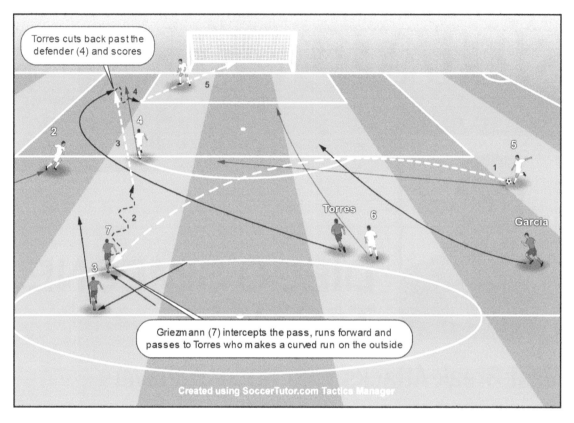

Torres cuts back past the defender (4) and scores

Griezmann (7) intercepts the pass, runs forward and passes to Torres who makes a curved run on the outside

In this situation the opposition centre back (5) tries to switch the play from left to right, but miss-hits his pass. The pass falls short and is intercepted by Griezmann (7) in the centre.

Griezmann (7) dribbles towards the box and Torres sprints across to make an overlapping run. The pass is played into the path of Torres who is closely followed by the other centre back (4). Torres checks back to avoid his marker and slots the ball past the goalkeeper.

The key to a successful transition from defence to attack in the centre is to play at high speed with positive runs into space - trying to finish the attack as quickly as possible while the opposition are still unbalanced.

SESSION FOR THIS TACTICAL SITUATION (3 PRACTICES)
1. Fast Break Attacks with Support Players in a 2 Zone Transition Game

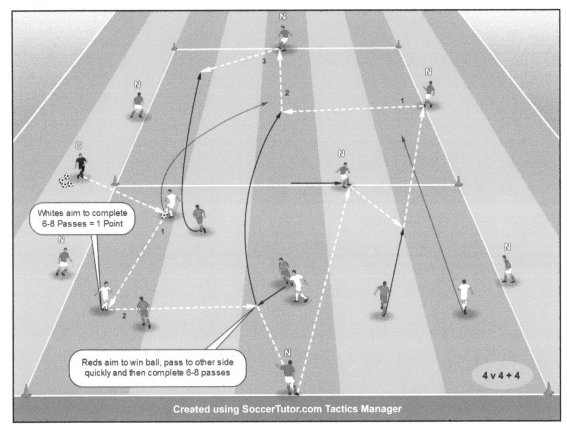

Whites aim to complete
6-8 Passes = 1 Point

Reds aim to win ball, pass to other side
quickly and then complete 6-8 passes

4 v 4 + 4

Created using SoccerTutor.com Tactics Manager

Objective: To develop the transition from defence to attack with quick support play.

Description

In a 20 x 30 yard area we split the pitch into 2 equal 20 x 15 yard zones. The red and white teams have 4 players each. There are also 7 blue neutral players in the positions shown, so that there are always 4 neutral players for each zone (1 on each side).

The practice starts with one team in possession (whites in diagram example). The objective is to complete 6-8 consecutive passes with the help of the 4 neutral players to score 1 point.

If the defending team (reds in diagram) win the ball, their objective is to pass the ball to the other side very quickly with the help of the neutral players - they then run into the opposite zone to maintain possession (support play). The practice continues as the whites also run into the opposite zone to try and win the ball back.

Coaching Point: Once a pass has been played to the other zone, the players must run quickly from behind to provide support, ask for the ball to be played into space and maintain possession for the team.

PROGRESSION

2. Fast Break Attacks and Finishing with Support Players in a 5 v 5 (+7) Transition Game

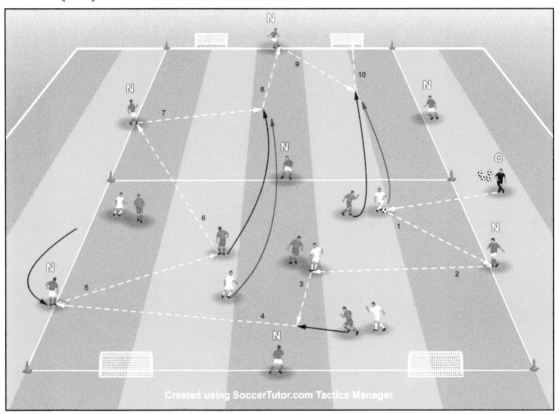

Description

For this progression of the previous practice we increase the size of the area to 25 x 40 yards and add 2 mini goals on each end line. Each team has 1 more player (5 v 5) and we have the same 7 blue neutral players.

If the defending team (reds in diagram) win the ball, their objective now is to move the ball quickly into the other zone, combine with the neutral players and then score in one of the mini goals.

The team that finishes their transition from defence to attack (reds in diagram) start the practice again in the other zone with possession of the ball. The same conditions apply with the team roles reversed. The other team (whites) then try to win the ball and score in the mini goals at the other end.

Coaching Point: Once a pass has been played to the other zone, the players must run quickly from behind to provide support, ask for the ball to be played into space and use controlled finishing to score.

PROGRESSION

3. Fast Break Attacks from the Middle Zone with Support Players in a Transition Game

The reds try to win the ball and then play with neutrals to score within 12 secs (13 v 6)

Created using SoccerTutor.com Tactics Manager

Description

In the final practice of this session we use a full pitch and create a central zone as shown in the diagram. Each team has 6 outfield players within the zone and 1 goalkeeper outside defending a full size goal. We also have 7 neutral support players (blues) - 1 inside, 1 on each side and 2 at each end of the zone.

The practice starts with one team in possession (whites in diagram) as they try to build up play and work the ball into the penalty area and score. The support players do not play with this team in the attacking phase.

If the defending team (reds in diagram) win the ball, they must make a quick transition from defence to attack with help from all 7 of the support players. Their aim is to use good and fast combination play to create a chance and score within 12 seconds.

Rules

1. The players can make runs out wide (outside the wide support players) when attacking. They can make overlap or under-lap runs.
2. All players are limited to 2 or 3 touches, but the support players only have 1 or 2 touches.

TACTICAL SITUATION 4

JOSE MOURINHO TACTICS

Exploiting a Numerical Advantage in the Centre with Fast Support Play

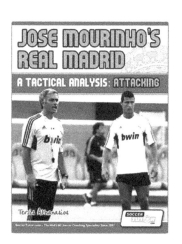

Analysis taken from 'Jose Mourinho's Real Madrid: A Tactical Analysis - Attacking in the 4-2-3-1' (Athanasios Terzis 2012)

Available to buy from SoccerTutor.com (paperback + eBook)

The analysis is based on recurring patterns of play. Once the same phase of play occurred a number of times (at least 10) the tactics would be decoded, with the positioning of each player on the pitch studied in great detail, including their body shape. Each individual movement with or without the ball was also recorded in detail. The analysis on the next page is an example of the team's tactics being used effectively.

The analysis is then used to create a full progressive session to coach this specific tactical situation.

Analysis taken from 'Jose Mourinho's Real Madrid: A Tactical Analysis - Attacking' (Athanasios Terzis)

Exploiting a Numerical Advantage in the Centre with Fast Support Play

In this situation, Xabi Alonso (14) intercepts the forward pass from the centre back. Alonso (14) is put under pressure immediately so passes inside to Khedira who has plenty of space.

The opposition's left winger (11) does not react quickly enough to block off the pass to Di Maria, so he is able to receive the pass from Khedira and moves towards the opposition's penalty area.

Benzema (option 1) and Ronaldo (option 2) make diagonal runs and are ready to receive passes into the penalty area as shown.

Di Maria (22) also has the opportunity to try and shoot at goal (option 3).

1. Possession with a Numerical Advantage and Fast Support in a Dynamic 2 Zone Game

Diagram 1: When the Blue Team Complete 6-8 Passes

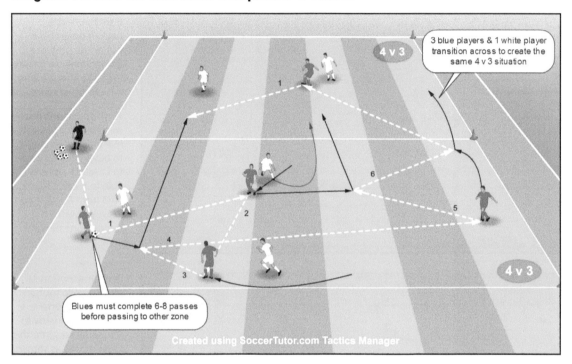

Objective: Developing possession play with a numerical advantage and fast support movements.

Description

In a 25 x 25 yard area we split the pitch into 2 equal zones. We have 2 teams with 5 players each.

We start the practice in one zone with a 4 v 3 numerical advantage for the team in possession (blues). In the other zone the blues start with a numerical disadvantage (1 v 2).

1. The first objective for the blue team is to keep the ball against the 3 white players and complete 5-6 consecutive passes.

2. If this happens, they can then pass to their lone teammate in the other zone. 3 blue players must then all run forward to support him quickly to maintain their numerical advantage and possession of the ball - 1 white player also moves across to recreate the same 4 v 3 and 1 v 2 situations in the 2 zones.

Diagram 2: When the White Team Win the Ball Before the Blues Complete 6-8 Passes

The whites win the ball

1 blue player swaps with a white player in the other zone so it is still 4 v 3 for the team in possession

Created using SoccerTutor.com Tactics Manager

This shows an alternative situation to diagram 1.

If the defending team (whites) win the ball before the blue team are able to complete 6-8 passes, 1 white player enters from the other zone and 1 blue player moves across to the other zone. This recreates the same 4 v 3 situation and the practice continues in the same way with the team roles reversed.

All players have unlimited touches / All players are limited to 2-3 touches.

Coaching Points

1. When out of possession, the team needs to close the space, limiting the time and options for the opposition, trying to force a mistake.

2. Once the ball is won, the players on that team then need to spread out to use all the space available to maintain possession.

3. When a team wins the ball, the player who joins from the other zone needs to do so very quickly. This is so that the team can utilise their new 4 v 3 numerical advantage as soon as possible, maximising their chance of maintaining possession of the ball.

PROGRESSION

2. Possession with a Numerical Advantage and Fast Support in a Dynamic Transition Game

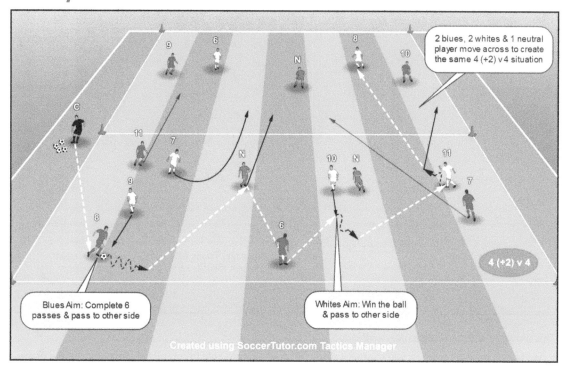

Description

In a 30 x 40 yard area we split the pitch into 2 equal zones (30 x 20 yards). We have 2 teams of 6 players each and 3 neutral players (reds).

In the first zone we have 4 blue midfielders, 2 red neutral players (who take the role of 2 forwards) and 4 white attackers. In the other zone we have 2 blue forwards, 2 white central midfielders and 1 neutral player.

The practice starts with the blue team in possession with a 4 (+2) v 4 situation. They aim to complete 6 consecutive passes with the help of the 2 neutral players to score 1 point.

As soon as the blues have completed 6 passes, they can pass to one of the 2 forwards in the other zone. If they are successful, 2 blue midfielders run forward to support the forwards. 2 white players and 1 neutral player also move into this zone to create the same 4 (+2) v 4 situation and the practice continues in the same way, but in the other zone.

The objective for the defending team (whites) is to press, win the ball and then quickly pass the ball to one of their teammates in the other zone. If this happens (as shown in the diagram), 2 white players run across to provide support and maintain possession. 2 blue players and 1 neutral player also move across to recreate the same 4 (+2) v 4 situation in the other zone, but with the team roles reversed. This practice is continuous.

3. Exploiting a Numerical Advantage in the Centre in a 4 Zone Transition Game

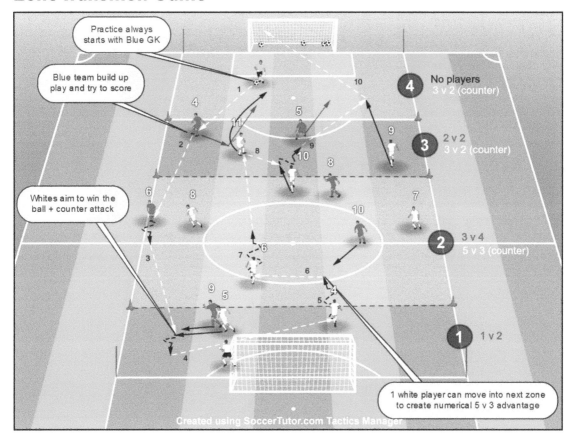

Practice always starts with Blue GK

Blue team build up play and try to score

Whites aim to win the ball + counter attack

No players
3 v 2 (counter)

4

2 v 2
3 v 2 (counter)

3

3 v 4
5 v 3 (counter)

2

1 v 2

1

1 white player can move into next zone to create numerical 5 v 3 advantage

Created using SoccerTutor.com Tactics Manager

Description

Mark out an area in between the 2 penalty areas with 4 zones, as shown in the diagram. The white team are in a 2-4-2 formation from the 4-4-2 with a diamond and the blue team are in a 2-2-1-1 formation from the 4-2-3-1.

The players keep within their zones in the first phase and contest their direct opponents. The blue team aim to build up play through the zones and score. The white team try to win the ball and then counter.

Phase 1: The practice always starts with the blue team's goalkeeper who passes to a centre back in zone 3 where there is a 2 v 2 situation. The blue team aim to pass into zone 2 where there is a 4 v 3 advantage for the whites. Finally, the blues aim to pass into zone 1 to their striker (9) and try to score (2 v 1 advantage for the whites).

Phase 2: The objective for the white team is to win the ball as quickly as possible and then launch a quick counter attack. For the counter attack, 1 white player can move forward into the next zone to create an overload.

In the diagram example, the whites win the ball in zone 1 and No.4 is able to move forward and create a 5 v 3 situation in zone 2. No.10 then moves forward into the next zone and there is a final 3 v 2 situation across zones 3 and 4 where the whites try to score. If the ball goes out of play, start again with the blue team's goalkeeper.

93

PROGRESSION

4. Blocking Passes Out Wide to Exploit a Numerical Advantage in the Centre (Zonal Transition Game)

Description

In this progression of the previous practice, we add side zones as shown in the diagram. We also add 2 white full backs (2 & 3), 2 blue full backs (2 & 3) and 2 blue wingers (7 & 11) who all operate in the side zones. The white team are in a 4-4-2 with a diamond midfield and the blue team are in a 4-2-3-1 formation.

The practice always starts with the blue team's goalkeeper who passes into the main zone. The blues build up and try to score, with the focus on playing the ball out wide where they have a 2 v 1 advantage in each side zone. The objective for the white team is to win the ball and then launch a quick break attack to score themselves. *See coaching points for full description of the white team's tactics.*

Coaching Points

1. The first objective for the white team is to win possession. They must draw the opposition (blues) into the centre by blocking passes out wide, where they will be outnumbered.
2. If the whites can force the play into the centre, then they can exploit their numerical advantage in there (4 v 3 in midfield) to win the ball and launch a fast break attack.
3. The transition from defence to attack must be fast with quick combination play and supporting runs.

TACTICAL SITUATION 5

PEP GUARDIOLA TACTICS

Fast Break Attacks Using Wide Players

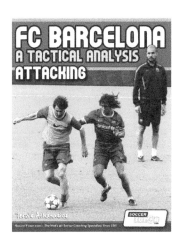

**Analysis taken from 'FC Barcelona: A Tactical Analysis - Attacking'
(Athanasios Terzis 2011)**

Available to buy from SoccerTutor.com (paperback + eBook)

The analysis is based on recurring patterns of play. Once the same phase of play occurred a number of times (at least 10) the tactics would be decoded, with the positioning of each player on the pitch studied in great detail, including their body shape. Each individual movement with or without the ball was also recorded in detail. The analysis on the next page is an example of the team's tactics being used effectively.

The analysis is then used to create a full progressive session to coach this specific tactical situation.

Analysis taken from 'FC Barcelona: A Tactical Analysis - Attacking' (Athanasios Terzis)

Fast Break Attacks Using Wide Players

Busquets (16) and Pedro (11) apply immediate pressure and dispossess the new ball carrier

In this example, the opposition centre back (4) attempts a forward pass towards No.11.

Busquets (16) and Pedro (11) apply immediate pressure and double mark the new ball carrier.

Busquets intercepts the ball.

Busquets (16) passes to Pedro (17) who runs into the space on the right and receives. He moves forward and crosses towards Iniesta (8) and Messi inside the box, while Xavi (6) takes up a position outside the penalty area.

Barca liked to double up on the man in possession, which meant that when they won the ball, they could immediately use this 2 v 1 situation to their advantage.

SESSION FOR THIS TACTICAL SITUATION (5 PRACTICES)
1. Fast Break Attacks and Quick Decision Making in a 2 v 1 (+1) Situation with 4 Goals

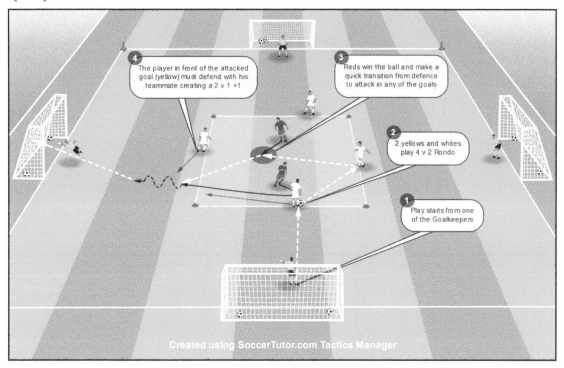

4 The player in front of the attacked goal (yellow) must defend with his teammate creating a 2 v 1 +1

3 Reds win the ball and make a quick transition from defence to attack in any of the goals

2 2 yellows and whites play 4 v 2 Rondo

1 Play starts from one of the Goalkeepers

Created using SoccerTutor.com Tactics Manager

Objective: Developing fast break attacks when the opposition are unorganised.

Description

In a 30 x 30 yard area we have 4 full size goals (1 on each side) with 4 goalkeepers. In the middle we mark out a smaller square (10 x 10 yards) and in this area we have 3 teams of 2 players each. There are 2 teams (yellow and white) outside the small square and one team (red) inside as we play a 4 v 2 rondo possession game.

When the defending pair (reds) win the ball, they must make a quick transition from defence to attack. They can attack any of the 4 goals. The player on that side defends the goal and his teammate tracks back to help - this is why we have a 2 v 1 (+1) situation. In this example the 2 reds win the ball and then attack the goal to the left against the 1 (+1) yellow players.

Coaching Points

1. This practice is about decision making and depends on the actions of the first defender:
   - The first attacker who wins the ball should try to draw the first defender towards him. If this happens he passes to his teammate in space.
   - If the defender decides instead to cover the second attacker, then the first attacker attacks the goal and tries to score himself.
2. The second attacker needs to be alert and time his run well to receive on the move. He should take a maximum of 2 touches to score - control and shoot.

97

PROGRESSION

2. Fast Break Attacks (4 v 2) in a Continuous 3 Team Game

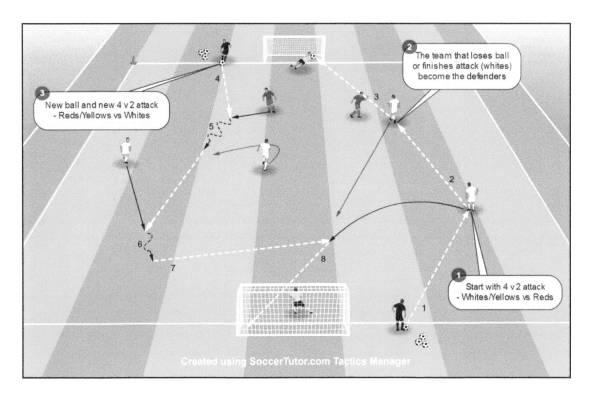

Objective: Developing fast break attacks with a numerical advantage.

Description

Within the same 30 x 30 yard area as the previous practice, we remove 2 of the goals and play a normal directional game. We have the same 3 teams of 2 players (red, yellow and white).

1. Two teams start the practice together by attacking against one team. In the diagram example, we have the yellows and whites attacking the reds.

2. As soon as the attack is finished, the coach immediately gives a new ball to the team that were defending (reds). The team that loses the ball or finishes an attack become the defending team (whites).

3. The reds make a quick transition from defence to attack and try to score. The other team (yellows) join the reds to create another 4 v 2 attack in the opposite direction, with the same aims and conditions.

The 2 white players must track back very quickly. This is a practice with continuous 4 v 2 attacks. You can add an extra pair or two to allow the players time to rest.

Coaching Points

1. When the coach passes the ball in for the transition from defence to attack, the player that receives should run forward with the ball at speed, drawing opponents in and beating them or create space for teammates to run into, before passing to them.

2. There should also be quick, quality and synchronised movements to finish the attacks effectively.

PROGRESSION

3. Fast Break Attacks and Quick Reactions in a Dynamic 6 Goal Game

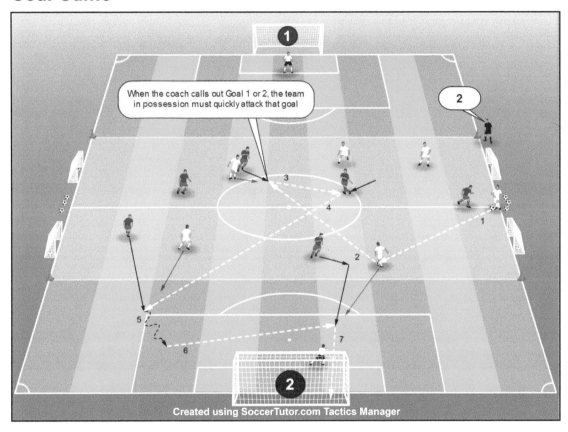

When the coach calls out Goal 1 or 2, the team in possession must quickly attack that goal

Objective: Developing fast break attacks within changing game situations.

Description

Using a full pitch, we mark out a central zone and position 4 mini goals on the sidelines as shown. We also have a full size goal with a goalkeeper at both ends of the pitch.

We start the practice with 2 teams (reds vs whites) playing a normal 6 v 6 small sided game within the central zone. The direction of play is using the width of the pitch as both teams defend 2 mini goals.

The players wait for the coach to shout out '1' or '2' which refers to each of the full size goals (numbered in diagram). The team that is in possession at the time must then change their direction of play and attack that goal. As soon as the coach gives this signal, all of the players are free to leave the central zone to attack/defend. The coach will most often shout out a goal number as soon as a team wins the ball from the opposition, thus starting a fast transition from defence to attack.

When the attack is finished or the ball goes out of play, both teams return to the central zone and we start playing 6 v 6 again, waiting for the coach's next signal.

PROGRESSION

4. Fast Break Attacks with Wide Players - Crossing and Finishing (1)

Red team try to win ball in 5 v 7 situation, pass out wide and then score

White team aim to complete 6-8 passes (1 point) or keep ball for 15 secs (2 points)

Created using SoccerTutor.com Tactics Manager

Description

Using a full pitch, we reduce the width of the playing area as shown in the diagram. We also mark out a central zone which is the width of the penalty area. Both teams have 9 outfield players and there are also 2 goalkeepers. There are 7 white players and 5 red players in the central zone. There are also 4 red players outside in wide positions with 1 white defender in each penalty box.

The practice starts in the central zone where the whites have a 7 v 5 numerical advantage and try to keep possession of the ball. If they complete 6-8 consecutive passes they score 1 point and if they keep the ball for 15 seconds, they score 2 points.

The objective for the 5 red players inside the central zone is to apply pressure and win the ball. They must then pass very quickly to one of the 4 red attackers outside the central zone. 2 red players can then leave the central zone and make runs into the penalty area to try and finish from an incoming cross against 1 white defender. A red goal scores 1 point but if a goal is scored directly from a cross, it is worth 2 points.

Progression: You can have 3 red players making runs into the penalty area against 2 white defenders.

Coaching Points

1. The team needs to defend well, limit the time and space their opponents have and press collectively.
2. Once the ball is won, the aim should be to quickly pass the ball out wide and then make quick supporting runs into the penalty area, ready for the cross.

PROGRESSION

5. Fast Break Attacks with Wide Players - Crossing and Finishing (2)

No.5 wins the ball & passes to No.8

Description

Using a full pitch, we mark out a central zone and 2 side zones with 2 full sized goals in the positions shown. Both teams have 9 players including goalkeepers. The red team are in a 2-2-3-1 formation (from 4-2-3-1) and the white team are in a 4-2-2 formation (from 4-4-2).

The red team's wide players (7 & 11) are positioned in the side zones and only play in the transition from defence to attack. They can move freely as soon as their team wins the ball. The white players are not allowed in the side zones at anytime.

The practice starts with the white team in possession trying to score. The objective for the red team is to defend with their numerical disadvantage (6 v 8) in the main zone, win the ball and then exploit their wide players to create goal scoring opportunities.

The red team (when in transition from defence to attack) should look to play to the wide players in behind the opponent's defensive line, so that they can play final balls or cross into the penalty area as quickly as possible. The red team should have 2 or 3 players from the central zone and the wide player on the opposite flank all making runs into the penalty area to try and finish the attack.

TACTICAL SITUATION 6

DIEGO SIMEONE TACTICS

Fast Break Attacks with Quick Combination Play in the Centre

Content taken from Analysis of Atlético Madrid during the 2014/2015 La Liga winning season

The analysis is based on recurring patterns of play observed within the Atlético Madrid team. Once the same phase of play occurred a number of times (at least 10) the tactics would be seen as a pattern. The analysis on the next page is an example of the team's tactics being used effectively, taken from a specific game.

Each action, pass, individual movement with or without the ball, and the positioning of each player on the pitch including their body shape, are presented.

The analysis is then used to create a full progressive session to coach this specific tactical situation.

Analysis Taken from 'Athletic Bilbao vs Atlético Madrid - 21 Dec 2014'
Fast Break Attacks with Quick Combination Play in the Centre

Tiago (5) tackles No.10 and passes to Garcia (8) who then makes a forward run and later receives from Turan

In this example Atlético Madrid had many players in a compact formation in the centre, limiting the time and space available for the opposition midfielders. The Bilbao No.10 is closed for space and is dispossessed by Tiago (5).

Atlético demonstrate great combination play in a tight space: Tiago (5) -> Garcia (8) -> Niguez -> Turan -> Garcia (8) and finally out wide to Juanfran who makes a run forward.

The right back Juanfran delivers a cross with many Atlético players making runs into the box. The cross is timed perfectly for Griezmann (7) to meet the ball and head it past the goalkeeper.

Atlético Madrid often squeezed the play in the centre to win the ball and then used their quick combination play to break through pressure and launch effective counter attacks.

SESSION FOR THIS TACTICAL SITUATION (3 PRACTICES)
1. Transition Play in a 4 (+3) v 4 Dynamic 2 Zone Possession Game (1)

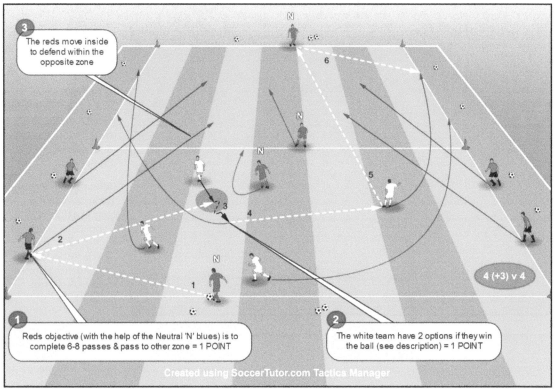

3 The reds move inside to defend within the opposite zone

1 Reds objective (with the help of the Neutral 'N' blues) is to complete 6-8 passes & pass to other zone = 1 POINT

2 The white team have 2 options if they win the ball (see description) = 1 POINT

4 (+3) v 4

Created using SoccerTutor.com Tactics Manager

Description

In a 30 x 40 yard area, we divide the pitch into 2 equal zones. We have 2 teams of 4 players (whites v reds) and 4 blue neutral players who play with the team in possession.

One team plays on the outside (reds) and starts in possession, trying to keep the ball with the 3 blue neutral players as shown in the diagram - this is a 4 (+3) v 4 situation.

The aim is to complete 6-8 consecutive passes (1 point) and then pass the ball to the neutral player in the other zone. All players quickly move across to take up the same positions (except for 1 neutral player who stays on the bottom end line) which creates the same 4 (+3) v 4 situation in the other zone. The objectives remain the same.

The aim for the defending team (whites) is to apply pressure and win the ball. They then have 2 options:

1. Pass to the neutral player in the other zone and run quickly to take up positions at the sides of that zone. The red players and 1 neutral player also move across to create the same 4 (+3) v 4 situation with the team roles reversed *(this is shown in the diagram example)*.

2. Pass to a neutral player within the same zone and run quickly to take up positions at the side of the same zone (swap with reds) - the teams switch roles and whites try to maintain possession with a 4 (+3) v 4 situation.

VARIATION

2. Transition Play in a 4 (+3) v 4 Dynamic 2 Zone Possession Game (2)

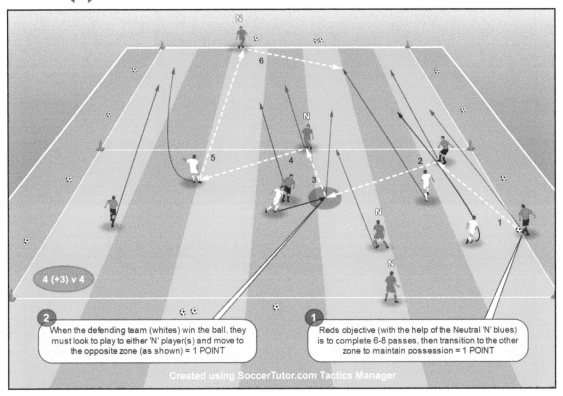

4 (+3) v 4

2 When the defending team (whites) win the ball, they must look to play to either 'N' player(s) and move to the opposite zone (as shown) = 1 POINT

1 Reds objective (with the help of the Neutral 'N' blues) is to complete 6-8 passes, then transition to the other zone to maintain possession = 1 POINT

Created using SoccerTutor.com Tactics Manager

Description

This is a variation of the previous practice in the same 30 x 40 yard area. All of the players should be midfielders or attackers.

This time both teams start within the zone. One team starts in possession (reds in diagram) with the help of 3 blue neutral players (1 inside / 2 outside) - this creates a 4 (+3) v 4 situation.

The rest of the practice works in exactly the same way as the previous practice, except when a team wins the ball they now always pass to the other zone and move across to keep possession. The team that loses the ball also moves across within the other zone to try and recover possession.

Variation: Remove 1 neutral player so we just have 1 on each line and add 1 player for each team so that we have 5 whites versus 5 reds within a zone.

Coaching Point: Once a pass has been played to the other zone, the players must run quickly from behind to provide support, ask for the ball to be played into space and maintain possession for the team.

PROGRESSION

3. Fast Break Attacks with Combination Play in the Centre (Position Specific Practice)

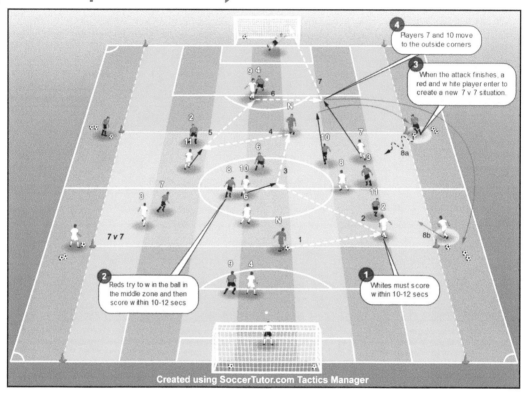

Created using SoccerTutor.com Tactics Manager

Description

In the final practice of this session we use a full pitch. As shown in the diagram, we mark out a central zone and 2 end zones. At each end of the central zone we have a blue neutral player who moves across the line, and plays the role of either a centre back or a forward.

Inside the central zone we play 7 v 7. Both teams have 2 full backs (2 & 3), 3 central midfielders (6, 8 & 10) and 2 wingers (7 & 11) from the 4-3-3 formation. In both end zones we have a 1 v 1 situation between 1 striker (9) and 1 centre back (4).

The practice starts with one of the blue neutral players. The team in possession (whites) try to score within 10-12 seconds. The objective for the defending team (reds) is to win the ball and launch a fast break attack, again finishing within 10-12 seconds. The players need to use quick combination play in the centre in a direct game.

The team in attack or transition from defence to attack must first pass to the neutral player in the forward role before then passing to the striker (9) in the end zone. The players from the central zone must then run into the end zone to provide support under pressure from their opponents and finish the attack quickly.

We have 1 player in each corner of the central zone. When the white attack finishes, 1 red player enters with a new ball and 1 white player also enters to create a new 7 v 7 situation immediately. The white team then need to make a quick transition from attack to defence. White No.7 and red No.10 move to an outside corner position.

CHAPTER 6

TRANSITION FROM DEFENCE TO ATTACK IN THE HIGH ZONE

TRANSITION FROM DEFENCE TO ATTACK IN THE HIGH ZONE

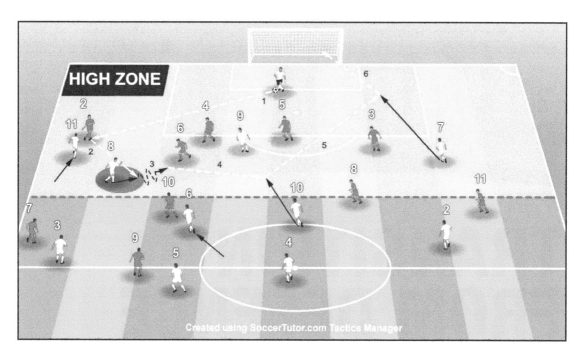

For this book, we have divided the chapters by which zone the transition starts in. There are 3 zones:

1. **Low Zone**

2. **Middle Zone**

3. High Zone

This diagram shows an example of a team that has won the ball in the high zone.

In this situation, the white team have players behind the ball when defending. To win the ball, they need to implement high pressing, close down the ball carrier, limit the opponent's time/space and block potential passing lanes with tight marking and good positioning.

In this example, the goalkeeper passes out wide to the red right back (2). As the white team are using a high press, there are limited passing options and limited time for the ball carrier to make a decision. The right back attempts a pass into the No.10, but it is intercepted by the white No.8 in an advanced position.

The white No.8 moves inside with the ball which draws in the white defensive midfielder (6). This creates space for the white No.10 to move forward and receive in space near the edge of the penalty area.

The white No.10 plays a good diagonal pass in between the red centre back (5) and left back (3). The right winger (7) makes a well timed run and scores with a first time shot.

The team in transition from defence to attack have limited time and space. The key to attacking in this situation from the high zone is to quickly pass into the opponent's box before other players are able to track back and recover. This requires good synchronisation between the weight of pass and the run in behind.

What is the Tactical Situation?

- Our team is high up the pitch and defending with many players in the opponent's half.

- We have a lot of space in behind our defensive line and often only have 2 players at the back.

- There is a short distance to the opponent's goal.

- We have many attacking options if we win the ball, but we have limited time and space.

- The opposition have many players in their own half of the pitch.

- There is little space to exploit in behind the opponent's defensive line.

- This tactical situation normally occurs with an equality in numbers.

What Objectives Should We Have?

- The basic aim is to win the ball by pressing the ball carrier and blocking off potential passing lanes.

- We must apply a high press and limit the opposition's space and time. We want to avoid our opponents playing a long pass in behind our defensive line or dribbling forward with the ball.

- Fast and quality attacking combinations are needed with good cooperation under pressure of time and space.

- We need to be aggressive and creative.

- Quickly pass into the opponent's penalty area with players making good runs.

- Synchronised movements in and around the penalty area to finish our attacks effectively and efficiently.

- To complete our attack within 4-8 seconds.

What Practices/Sessions Can We Create for this Tactical Situation?

- Defensive organisation and synchronised movements with an emphasis on high pressing within the high zone.

- Fast break attacks - we need to practice making the transition from defence to attack as quickly as possible. You should emphasise that the players should look to finish their attacks within a maximum time of 8 seconds.

TACTICAL SITUATION 1

CLAUDIO RANIERI TACTICS

Pressing High Up the Pitch and Fast Break Attack (1)

Content taken from Analysis of Leicester City FC during the 2015/2016 Premier League winning season

The analysis is based on recurring patterns of play observed within the Leicester City team. Once the same phase of play occurred a number of times (at least 10) the tactics would be seen as a pattern. The analysis on the next page is an example of the team's tactics being used effectively, taken from a specific game.

Each action, pass, individual movement with or without the ball, and the positioning of each player on the pitch including their body shape, are presented.

The analysis is then used to create a full progressive session to coach this specific tactical situation.

Analysis Taken from 'Everton FC vs Leicester City FC - 19 Dec 2015'

Pressing High Up the Pitch and Fast Break Attack (1a)

In this example, the opposition have a throw-in within their defensive third. Claudio Ranieri's team are positioned high up the pitch to mark their opponents tightly, and stop them from playing out.

The right back (2) throws the ball inside to the defensive midfielder (6) who attempts to pass back to the right back. Leicester's left winger Albrighton is able to move forward and intercept the pass.

Albrighton's touch drops to Vardy who runs inside with the ball. Okazaki makes a good run into the box and the opposition's centre back (4) has to try and contest Vardy. This enables Vardy to play a pass into Okazaki's path, who finishes into the bottom corner.

When Leicester won the ball high up the pitch, their aim was always to play the ball in behind and into the penalty area quickly as possible.

Analysis Taken from 'Leicester City FC vs Crystal Palace - 24 Oct 2015'

Pressing High Up the Pitch and Fast Break Attack (1b)

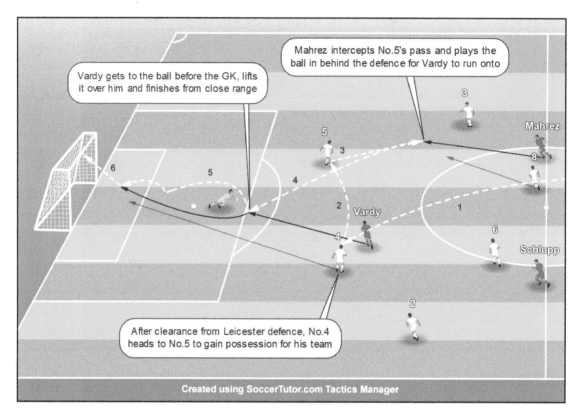

Mahrez intercepts No.5's pass and plays the ball in behind the defence for Vardy to run onto

Vardy gets to the ball before the GK, lifts it over him and finishes from close range

After clearance from Leicester defence, No.4 heads to No.5 to gain possession for his team

Created using SoccerTutor.com Tactics Manager

In this second example, Leicester have cleared the ball from defence into the opposition's half. Schlupp, Mahrez and Vardy run forward to limit the time their opponents have on the ball and try to force a mistake.

The centre back (4) is able to head the clearance to his centre back partner No.5. Leicester's right winger Mahrez anticipates the next pass being directed to the left back (3) and intercepts the pass. He then plays a pass in behind the defensive line for Vardy to run onto.

Vardy is quick enough to get to the ball before the goalkeeper, lift the ball over him and then score from close range under pressure from No.4.

As in the last example (1a), this also shows that when Leicester won the ball high up the pitch, their aim was always to play the ball in behind and into the penalty area as quickly as possible.

1. Possession and Transition Play in a Dynamic 4 Grid Game with 8 Mini Goals

Blues aim to win the ball & pass to a neutral player in another grid and then score a goal (2 points)

Whites aim to complete 6-8 passes within the grid (1 point), pass to a neutral player in another grid and then score a goal (2 points)

Created using SoccerTutor.com Tactics Manager

Objective: Developing possession and transition play with fast finishing under pressure of time and space.

Description

In a 40 x 40 yard area we divide the pitch into 4 equal grids. We have 8 mini goals in the positions shown and play with 2 teams of 5 and 4 neutral players (1 in each grid). The practice starts in one grid with one team in possession (whites in diagram) which creates a 5 (+1) v 5 situation.

The objective for the white team is to complete 6-8 consecutive passes (1 point) and then pass to a neutral player in one of the other 3 grids. All of the players can then move to that grid and try to score in a mini goal (2 points). The objective for the defending team (blues in diagram example) is to apply pressure in one grid, win the ball, change the direction of play by passing to a neutral player in another grid and score in a mini goal (2 points).

Rules

1. When an attack is finished or the ball goes out of play, the practice starts again in a different grid with the other team in possession.
2. If a team scores in all 8 of the mini goals they automatically become the winners of the game.

Progression: For a goal to count, all of that team's players have to have already moved into that grid. This forces all the players to react quickly in the transition from defence to attack.

2. Possession and Transition Play in a 6 v 4 (+6) Dynamic Game with 4 Goals

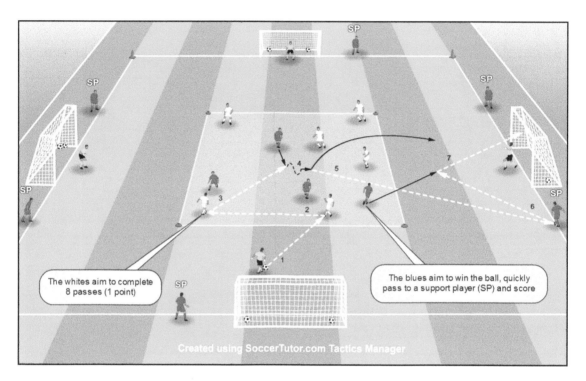

The whites aim to complete 8 passes (1 point)

The blues aim to win the ball, quickly pass to a support player (SP) and score

Created using SoccerTutor.com Tactics Manager

Description

In a 50 x 50 yard area, we mark out a central zone which is 18 x 18 yards. We have a full size goal with a goalkeeper on all 4 sides as shown. There are 6 white players and 4 blue players in the central zone. Outside the main area (next to the goals) we have an additional 6 blue support players in the positions shown.

The practice starts with a keeper's pass into the central zone with the white team in possession and the 4 blue players defending. The objective for the 6 white players is to maintain possession and complete 8 consecutive passes to score 1 point. The objective for the 4 blue players is to win the ball and pass to one of the blue outside support players (SP). They the make a fast transition from defence to attack, trying to score in any of the 4 goals.

Rules

1. Central zone - the white players are limited to 2-3 touches and the blue players have unlimited touches.
2. Central zone - the blue players must pass the ball to a support player within 4 seconds of winning the ball.
3. Outside zone - the blue players are limited to 1 or 2 touch finishing.
4. Outside zone - the blue support players are limited to 1 or 2 touches.

Coaching Points

1. The players need to be aggressive - quickly pass to a support player and then make positive runs.
2. Push the players to complete the attacks within 4-8 seconds.

PROGRESSION

3. Pressing High Up the Pitch and Fast Break Attacks in a Dynamic Transition Game (1)

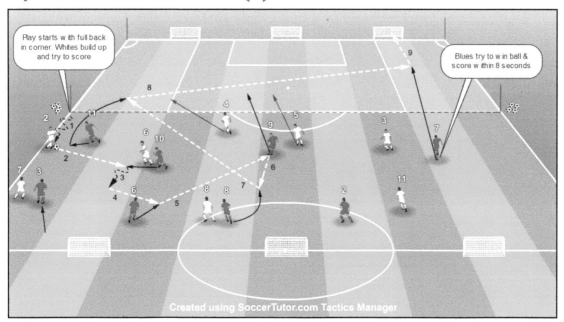

Description

Using half a pitch we create 2 zones as shown in the diagram - the zones are split along the line of the penalty area. We position 3 mini goals on the halfway line and another 3 mini goals on the end line. We play 8 v 8. The white team are in a 4-4 formation and the blue team are in a 2-2-3-1, 2-4-1-1 or 2-3-3 formation.

The practice starts with one of the white full backs (2 or 3) in the corner and the white team in possession within the larger zone. No players are allowed in the end zone in this phase. The white team try to score in one of the 3 mini goals on the halfway line (1 point).

The blue team defend and press high, trying to create a strong side and a numerical advantage around the ball. As soon as the blues win the ball, they launch a fast break attack. All the players in the practice (blues and whites) are then allowed to enter the end zone to defend/attack.

In the diagram example, the blue attacking midfielder (10) intercepts the pass towards white No.6. The blue team then launch a fast break attack and try to score in one of the mini goals (1 point). The whites move back to stop the blues and defend their 3 goals.

Rules

1. The white players have unlimited touches and the blue players are limited to 3 touches.
2. After the blue team win the ball, they must pass the ball into the end zone within 5 seconds.
3. If the blue team score within 6-8 seconds of winning the ball, the goal counts double.
4. The blue team must score from within the end zone.

4. Pressing High Up the Pitch and Fast Break Attacks in a Dynamic Transition Game (2)

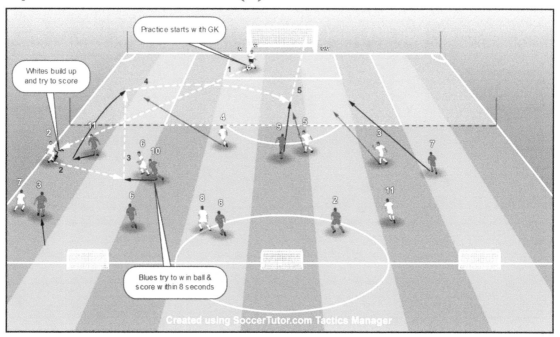

Practice starts with GK

Whites build up and try to score

Blues try to win ball & score within 8 seconds

Created using SoccerTutor.com Tactics Manager

Description

This is the same as the previous practice, but we remove the 3 mini goals from the end line. The team who make the transition from defence to attack (blues) now attack and try to score in a full size goal with a goalkeeper.

The practice now starts with the white team's goalkeeper passing to a teammate in the larger zone.

In this example, the blue No.10 gets in front of the opposition defensive midfielder (6) to win the ball and then passes to the left winger (11) to launch the fast break attack.

Rules

The rules are the same as the previous practice except:

1. If the whites complete 6 consecutive passes within the larger zone they get 1 point.
2. If the whites score in one of the 3 mini goals they get 2 points.

Coaching Points

1. There needs to be good defensive organisation and synchronised movements with an emphasis on high pressing within the high zone.
2. We are working on fast break attacks - we need to practice making the transition from defence to attack as quickly as possible. You should emphasise that the players should look to finish their attacks within a maximum time of 8 seconds.

5. Pressing High Up the Pitch and Fast Break Attacks in a Dynamic Transition Game (3)

Enter the zone = 1 Point
Score a goal = 3 Points

Created using SoccerTutor.com Tactics Manager

Description

In this variation of the previous 2 practices, we remove the 3 mini goals from the halfway line and mark out a 10 yard zone as shown.

We add another full size goal. The whites now try to score past the goalkeeper in the first phase.

Rules

The rules are the same as the previous practice except:

1. If the whites enter the 10 yard zone, they get 1 point.
2. If the whites score a goal they get 3 points.

TACTICAL SITUATION 2

PEP GUARDIOLA TACTICS

Pressing High Up the Pitch and Fast Break Attack (2)

Analysis taken from 'FC Barcelona: A Tactical Analysis - Attacking'
(Athanasios Terzis 2011)

Available to buy from SoccerTutor.com (paperback + eBook)

The analysis is based on recurring patterns of play. Once the same phase of play occurred a number of times (at least 10) the tactics would be decoded, with the positioning of each player on the pitch studied in great detail, including their body shape. Each individual movement with or without the ball was also recorded in detail. The analysis on the next page is an example of the team's tactics being used effectively.

The analysis is then used to create a full progressive session to coach this specific tactical situation.

Analysis taken from 'FC Barcelona: A Tactical Analysis - Attacking' (Athanasios Terzis)

Pressing High Up the Pitch and Fast Break Attack (2)

No.6 is immediately triple marked amd Xavi intercepts the ball

In this situation the opposition are attempting to build up play from the back.

The white centre back tries to direct a pass to No.6 who is in the centre of the pitch.

No.6 is immediately triple marked by Villa, Iniesta (8) and Xavi (6). Xavi intercepts the ball.

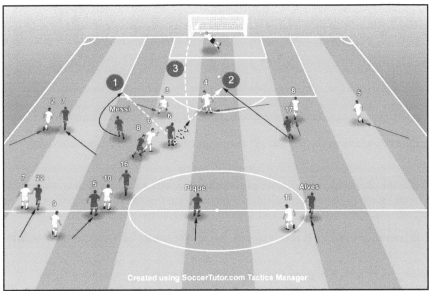

As the 2 opposing centre backs move towards the centre, Xavi (6) has 3 options:

1. The pass to Messi (10) is a very easy one.

2. Run forward with the ball and pass to Pedro (17).

3. Run forward with the ball and shoot at goal.

With Barcelona pressing so high up the pitch, the rewards are great when they win possession as the final ball can be played very quickly.

SESSION FOR THIS TACTICAL SITUATION (5 PRACTICES)
1. Possession and Transition Play in a 6 (+2) v 6 Dynamic Game

When the defending team (reds) win the ball, they swap positions with the whites and then try to keep possession

Created using SoccerTutor.com Tactics Manager

Objective: We work on applying pressure to win the ball and then maintaining possession after winning it.

Description

In a 10 x 20 yard area we divide the pitch into 2 equal zones and we have 2 teams of 6 players with an 2 extra neutral players. One team (white) starts in possession with all of their players at the sides of the pitch (in the positions shown in the diagram). There are 3 red players and 1 neutral player (yellow) inside each zone.

The objective for the team in possession (whites) is to complete 8 consecutive passes with help from the neutral players (1 point).

The objective for the defending team (reds) is to press and win the ball, then make a quick transition from defence to attack. As soon as the reds win the ball, they swap with the white players on the outside. The team roles are reversed and the reds try to maintain possession with the yellow neutral players.

Out of Possession = *CLOSE* the Space / In Possession = *OPEN* the space.

Rule: All players are limited to 2 or 3 touches except the neutral players who are limited to 1 or 2 touches.

PROGRESSION

2. Possession and Fast Break Attacks in a Dynamic Transition Game with Support Players

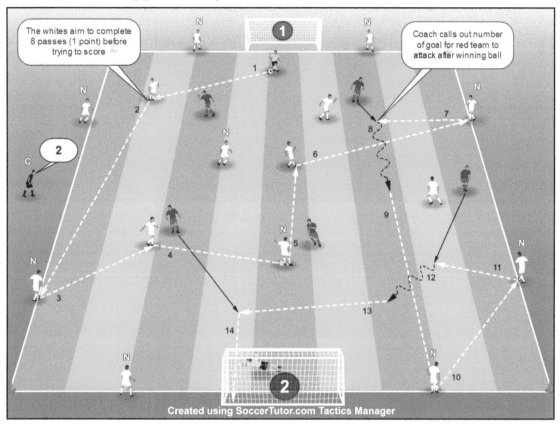

The whites aim to complete 8 passes (1 point) before trying to score

Coach calls out number of goal for red team to attack after winning ball

Created using SoccerTutor.com Tactics Manager

Description

In a 35 x 45 yard area we have 2 full size goals which are numbered 1 and 2 and a total of 22 players. There are 2 teams of 5 players (whites and reds), 10 neutral support players (yellows) and 2 goalkeepers.

Scenario 1: The practice starts with a keeper passing to the white team and their objective is to complete 8 passes (1 point). Once they complete 8 passes, the coach calls out which goal to attack and they try to score. If the reds win the ball, they must first complete 8 passes before trying to score in the goal called out by the coach.

Scenario 2 (Diagram): This is the same as scenario 1 for the first phase, but now when a team wins the ball, the coach calls out a number and that team launches an immediate fast break attack towards that goal. With this scenario, one team always starts with the aim of keeping possession and then scoring (whites). The other team (reds) always start in the defensive phase, trying to win the ball before scoring with a fast break attack.

Rules

1. The players have unlimited touches (or 2-3 touches) but the neutral players are limited to 1 touch.
2. The team which makes the transition from defence to attack (reds) must finish their attack within 8 seconds.

VARIATION

3. High Intensity Transition Play in a Small Sided Game with Support Players

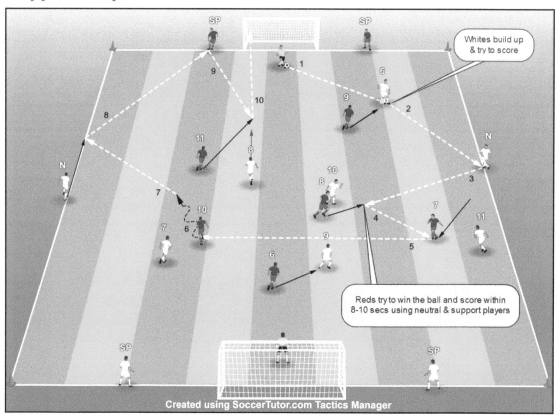

Description

Within the same 35 x 45 yard area as the previous practice, we remove 2 of the side players. Both teams have 5 outfield players inside the playing area - 3 central midfielders (6, 8 & 10), 2 wingers (7 & 11), a striker (9) and 2 outside support players (SP) either side of the goal. There are also 2 yellow neutral support players who move along the sidelines, who only play with the team in possession.

The practice starts with one team's keeper (whites in diagram) and that team try to score a goal with help from the neutral and support players. The objective for the defending team (reds) is to win the ball and then make a fast transition from defence to attack with help from the neutral and support players, trying to score a goal within 8-10 seconds.

Rules

1. Inside players have unlimited touches (or 3 touches), neutral players have 2 touches and support players have 1 touch.

2. The team that starts in possession (whites) have unlimited time to finish their attack, but the team in transition from defence to attack (reds) must finish their attack within 8-10 seconds.

PROGRESSION

4. High Press and Fast Transition to Attack in an 8 v 8 Tactical Game (1)

The empty goal forces the red team to press high

After winning the ball, the red team try to score within 6 secs

Created using SoccerTutor.com Tactics Manager

Description

Using a full pitch, we mark out the area shown in the diagram (10 yards beyond halfway line) and we have 2 full size goals with goalkeepers at either end. The red team have 8 players without a goalkeeper in a 2-3-3 formation (from 4-3-3) and the white team have 7 outfield players with a goalkeeper in a 2-2-3 formation (from 4-2-3-1).

The practice always starts with the white team's goalkeeper and the white team build up play and try to score (1 point). The red team have a numerical advantage (8 v 7) and press the ball to try and win it. If the reds are successful, they then try to exploit their numerical superiority in the transition from defence to attack and score past the goalkeeper (1 point) as quickly as possible, while the white team are still unorganised.

As the reds are defending a goal without a goalkeeper, they are forced to perform a quick high press on the ball carrier and the area around him - blocking off all passing options and trying to win the ball. Also, if the reds lose the ball after winning it, having no goalkeeper forces them to make the transition from attack to defence much more quickly.

Rules

1. If the white team complete 8 consecutive passes before scoring, the goal counts double (2 points).
2. If the reds score within 6 seconds of winning the ball, the goal counts double (2 points).

PROGRESSION

5. High Press and Fast Transition to Attack in an 8 v 8 Tactical Game (2)

Whites: Pass into this zone = 1 point
Score a goal = 2 points

Created using SoccerTutor.com Tactics Manager

Description

In this progression of the previous practice, we now use the full width of the pitch and create a 10 yard zone in the position shown.

We play an 11 v 11 game. Two centre backs are added for the red team (4-3-3 formation). Two full backs and a striker are added for the white team (4-2-3-1 or 4-4-1-1 formation).

We have the same objectives and rules as the previous practice except:

• If the white team successfully pass in behind the red team's defence (into the small 10 yard zone) they get 1 point.
• If the white team score a goal they get 2 points.

Coaching Points

1. The first basic aim for the red team is to win the ball by pressing the ball carrier and blocking off potential passing lanes.
2. Once the ball is won (transition from defence to attack), the red team should look to play the ball into the penalty area as quickly as possible, while the white team's defence is still unorganised.

TACTICAL SITUATION 3

DIEGO SIMEONE TACTICS

Pressing High Up the Pitch and Fast Break Attack (3)

Analysis taken from Analysis of Atlético Madrid during the 2013/2014 La Liga winning season

The analysis is based on recurring patterns of play observed within a team. Once the same phase of play occurred a number of times (at least 10) the tactics would be seen as a pattern. The analysis on the next page is an example of the team's tactics being used effectively, taken from a specific game.

Each action, pass, individual movement with or without the ball, and the positioning of each player on the pitch including their body shape, are presented.

The analysis is then used to create a full progressive session to coach this specific tactical situation.

Pressing High Up the Pitch and Fast Break Attack (3)

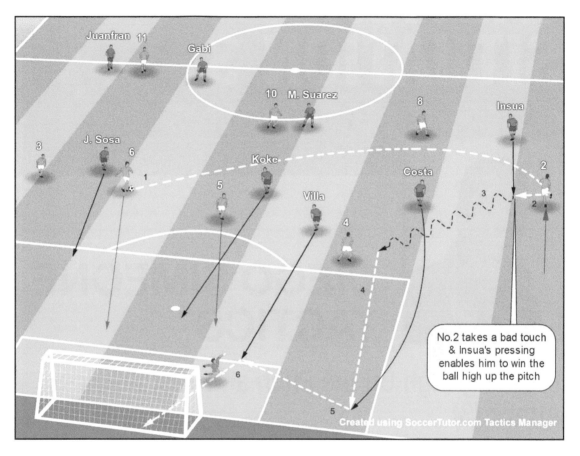

No.2 takes a bad touch & Insua's pressing enables him to win the ball high up the pitch

In this example, Atlético Madrid have 7 players in the opposition half to prevent the opposition from building up play and try to win the ball.

The right midfielder José Sosa closes down the opposition's defensive midfielder (6) and stops him from passing towards the left. This forces No.6 to play a long pass towards the right side.

The opposition's right back (2) struggles to control the ball under pressure and takes a bad first touch. Atlético's left back Insua moves forward to win the ball and then carries the ball towards the penalty area. As the centre back (4) has to contest Insua, Costa is able to make an overlapping run into the space in behind and receive the next pass inside the penalty area.

Costa passes to the near post where Villa has made a run in between the 2 centre backs to finish.

SESSION FOR THIS TACTICAL SITUATION (4 PRACTICES)
1. Dynamic 5 (+1) v 5 Transition Game with 4 Empty Goals

Blues aim to complete 6-8 passes

The coach calls out number of goal to attack when reds win the ball

Created using SoccerTutor.com Tactics Manager

Description

In a 35 x 35 yard are we have 4 empty goals (randomly numbered) positioned on each side. We play 5 v 5 with 1 additional neutral player (yellow) who always plays with the team in possession.

Scenario 1: The practice starts with the blues and their first aim is to complete 6-8 consecutive passes (1 point). Once they complete 6-8 passes, the coach calls out which goal to attack and they try to score. If the reds win the ball, they must first complete 6-8 consecutive passes and then try to score in the goal called out by the coach. *This scenario is not shown in the diagram above.*

Scenario 2: This is the same as scenario 1 for the first phase, but now the coach only calls out a number of a goal when a team wins the ball. That team then launches an immediate fast break attack towards the goal called out. When the attack finishes, the practice starts again, with the team that just finished their attack in possession.

Scenario 3: One team (blues) always start the practice with the aim of keeping possession and then scoring. The other team (reds) always start in the defensive phase, trying to win the ball, before scoring with a fast break attack.

Variation: In all scenarios, the coach can call a second number to change the direction of an active attack.

Rule: All players have unlimited touches (or 2-3 touches) and neutral players are limited to 1 or 2 touches.

VARIATION

2. Dynamic 5 (+2) v 5 Transition Game with 4 Goals + Keepers

Created using SoccerTutor.com Tactics Manager

Description

In this variation of the previous practice, we extend the area to 40 x 40 yards. We also add a goalkeeper in each of the 4 goals and an extra neutral player.

All of the same objectives and rules from the previous practice apply again here.

Coaching Points

1. As soon as the ball is won, the first pass should be to a player free in space. This will enable that player time to pick the right direction to launch the attack.

2. The transition from defence to attack (from the time the ball is won to a shot on goal) should take a maximum of 8 seconds.

PROGRESSION

3. Transition Play in a 6 (+2) v 6 (+2) Small Sided Game

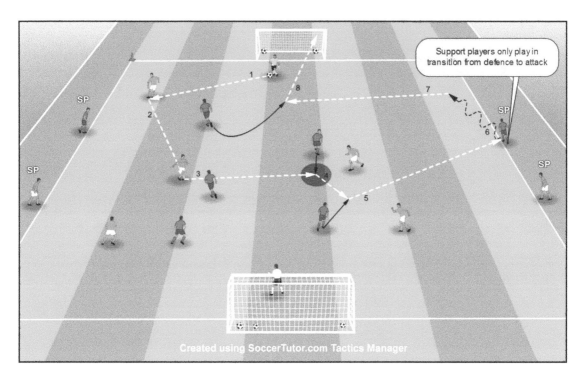

Support players only play in transition from defence to attack

Created using SoccerTutor.com Tactics Manager

Description

In this progression of the previous 2 practices, both teams now defend 1 goal each. We play 5 v 5 inside the area again but we remove the neutral players. Both teams have 2 support players instead (1 outside the area on each side, as shown in the diagram).

The support players only play when their team is in transition from defence to attack which creates a numerical advantage for this tactical situation.

One team's goalkeeper starts with the ball and that team (blues in diagram example) try to score. The defending team (reds) try to win the ball. When this happens, the aim is to make a quick transition from defence to attack with help from the outside support players. The outside players can enter the pitch but cannot score.

When the attack is finished, the practice starts again with the goalkeeper of the team which finished the last attack.

Rules

1. The support players can enter the pitch as soon as there is a transition from defence to attack for their team.
2. The support players are not allowed to score.
3. All players have unlimited touches but the support players are limited to 2 or 3 touches.
4. If a team scores a goal with a normal attack, they get 1 point.
5. If a team scores a goal with a successful transition from defence to attack, they get 2 points.

129

PROGRESSION

4. High Press and Fast Transition to Attack in a Dynamic 4 Zone Game

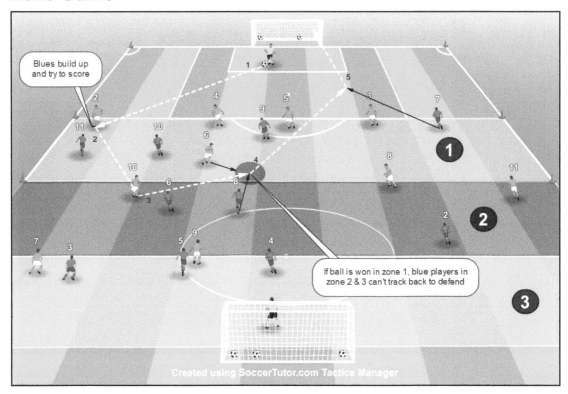

Description

In the final practice of this session, we use a full pitch. We mark out an area 15 yards beyond the halfway line and create 3 equal sized zones (1, 2 & 3) as shown in the diagram.

We play a normal 11 v 11 game. The blue team are in a 4-4-2 or 4-4-1-1 formation and the red team are in a 4-3-3 formation. The practice always starts with the blue team's goalkeeper who must pass to a blue player in zone 1 and the blue team build up play and try to score a goal.

The objective for the red team is to apply high pressing and win the ball. If they are successful, they then need to make a very quick transition from defence to attack. They try and score as soon as possible while the opposition's defence is still unbalanced.

Zone Rules

1. The zone in which the red team wins the ball has significance. When the reds win the ball in a zone e.g. Zone 1 (as shown in the diagram), the blue players behind in zones 2 and 3 are not allowed to track back and defend. The red players therefore attack against the blue players left in zone 1 only.

2. No players are allowed outside of the 3 zones in the first phase but the reds are free to move anywhere once they win the ball. The blue players (defending team) are not allowed to move into the end/final zone in the transition until the ball is played in there.

THE TRANSITION FROM ATTACK TO DEFENCE

CHAPTER 7

TECHNICAL & TACTICAL REQUIREMENTS IN THE TRANSITION FROM ATTACK TO DEFENCE

COACHING THE TRANSITION FROM ATTACK TO DEFENCE

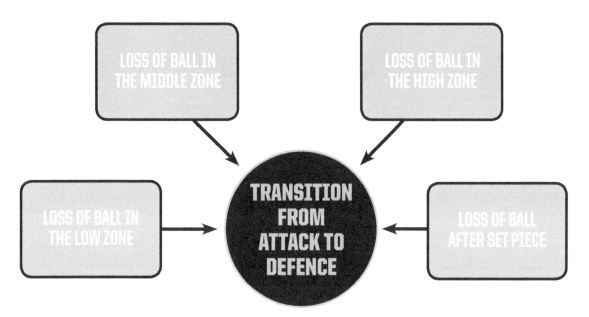

In this phase of the game we should first and foremost think about where and how we start our attack and what attacking style we want to implement.

We can then determine what positioning and reactions we will need for the transition from attack to defence.

We must then work on all the possible tactical situations in the transition from attack to defence repeatedly in training, so we are ready for all potential tactical situations in our competitive matches.

Based on this, every coach should be targeting his team's training on the possible loss of the ball in all zones of the pitch (low, middle and high zones).

We then work on how we want to defend, based on what kind of players we have in our team and what kind of players the opposition have. We must utilise the individual strengths of our players and as a group, against the weaknesses of our opponents.

TRANSITION FROM ATTACK TO DEFENCE FLOW CHART

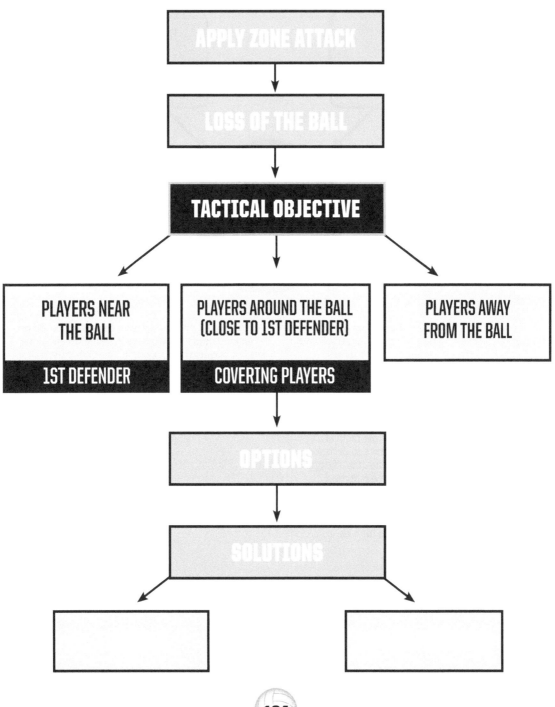

Apply Zone Attack

We must decide which zone to build up our attacking game. Where and how do we consolidate possession of the ball, how do we penetrate the opposition defence and how do we finish our attack as a team?

The zone we decide to attack from depends on our tactical/technical characteristics and formation against our opponent.

Loss of the Ball

We must decide which zone and area of the pitch our team can afford to lose the ball. This requires having good positioning while in possession, to prepare for the negative transition.

Tactical Objective

What are the tactical objectives that we have in this situation as individuals, as a group and as a whole team?

Decision Making

- The player nearest to the ball when we lose it must press the new ball carrier - where, how, when?

- The other players closest to the ball - should they press the ball, mark the potential receivers tightly or cover space?

- The players away from the ball - what movements should they make? - Where, how, when?

Options

What are the basic objectives and options in all of these situations and how can we work to avoid our opponents taking advantage when we lose the ball?

Solutions

What solutions do we have and how can we be most effective in this situation? (We can provide the players with solutions for each situation in training).

Opportunities

What are the opportunities in these tactical situations and how can we exploit them to get the best results?

Threats

What are the threats we must pay attention to which the opposition may be able to exploit?

TECHNICAL REQUIREMENTS

- When defending, use a staggered stance, alternating front and back foot.

- Feet shoulder width apart, legs bent, arched over, on your toes (don't get flat-footed).

- Feints and stabs but do not fully commit until the ball carrier makes a mistake.

- Concentrate on the player, not the ball, and look at his hips, not his feet or upper body.

- Keep an eye on the space between the ball and the ball carrier. If the ball gets away from their feet, step in to win possession.

- Close the distance between yourself and the ball carrier. Get close enough to force him to alter his course of attack and to force his head down to concentrate on not losing possession of the ball.

- Choose the angle of approach to guide/force the ball carrier away from dangerous areas and spaces.

- Deny the player space to run into and penetrate.

- Prevent the player from shooting at goal. Block any attempted shot.

- If the ball carrier allows the ball to get in between his feet then step in to make a tackle.

- Tackles should be fully committed through the centre of the ball.

TACTICAL REQUIREMENTS

- Balanced positioning in the possession phase with small distances between the players and the midfield and defensive lines.

- The transition from attack to defence comes after we are in possession, so we will usually have at least 3 players around the ball.

- The goal is to win the ball back, not just force the ball carrier back.

- The whole team presses aggressively and in unison to win the ball back. Players step towards the ball.

- Move quickly to close down opponents with well-rehearsed, coordinated pressing by 2 or more players.

- Limit the ball carrier's time, space and options to pass or dribble the ball forward.

- Force the ball to be played in a specific direction (wide) to create and exploit a numerical advantage around the ball area.

- Get compact in width and depth. Intelligent positioning is needed to restrict space for the opposition to pass and move into.

- The player nearest the ball is **"The 1st Defender"**. Their role is to slow down the attack, not necessarily win the ball. They should prevent the ball being played forward. This pressure will cause the ball carrier's head down, making him concentrate on keeping control of the ball, so he is unable to look for passing options.

- The player(s) further away from the ball get into position to intercept all passing options and provide cover.

- The players can leave the most difficult and longest passing options provided there is good pressure and cover on the ball carrier and his nearest passing options.

- The first defender should not run straight at the ball carrier, but should come in at an angle that would force the ball carrier to pass back or to attack towards our covering defenders or towards the sideline. This makes the opponent's attack predictable and easy to read for covering defenders.

- Once the ball carrier has been contained and delayed, the first defender may move in closer to challenge for the ball, as he has sufficient cover.

- If the first defender can force the ball carrier to go backwards, he must maintain close pressure to prevent him from opening up space.

- The defence should use this opportunity to push forward as well, compressing the attack away from their goal.

- If there is no pressure on the ball carrier, then the defence do not push up as the player will have time and space to find and take advantage of the space in behind the defensive line. The players need to recognise the situation to determine when to press and when to track back to defend behind the ball.

- **"The 2nd Defender"** (the second closest to the ball) marks the player who is the nearest passing option. They must cover the space behind their teammate who is pressuring the ball. However, if there is a numerical advantage, he might decide to risk double teaming the ball carrier to win the ball back quickly.

- **"The 3rd Defender"** provides balance by covering the space (blocking passes) which could be exploited by the opponent to switch their point of attack e.g. by playing a long pass to the opposite wing.

- The team need to work effectively in a situation with a numerical disadvantage or equality in numbers.

- The strong side and the easiest/nearest path to goal needs to be protected.

- The team needs to also protect the weak side with quick reactions and switch the point (direction) of defence if necessary.

CHAPTER 8

TRANSITION FROM ATTACK TO DEFENCE IN THE LOW ZONE

TRANSITION FROM ATTACK TO DEFENCE IN THE LOW ZONE

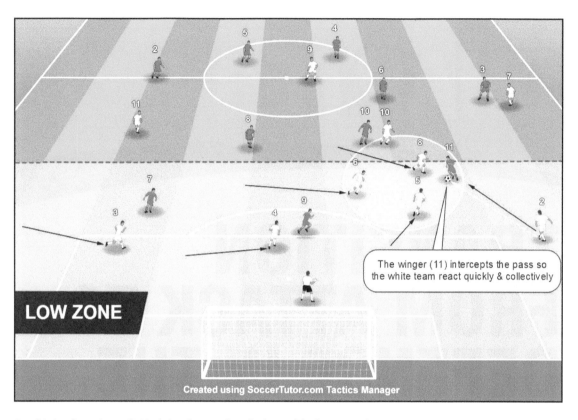

The winger (11) intercepts the pass so the white team react quickly & collectively

LOW ZONE

Created using SoccerTutor.com Tactics Manager

For this book, we have divided the chapters by which zone the transition starts in. There are 3 zones:

1. Low Zone

2. **Middle Zone**

3. **High Zone**

This diagram shows an example of a team that has lost the ball in the low zone. In this situation, the white team are building up play from the back and the opposition winger (11) intercepts the pass from the full back (2). The white team are temporarily unbalanced so the players must shift across or track back to close the spaces available (as shown in the diagram).

It is important that pressure is applied to the new ball carrier immediately, before he is able to get his head up to dribble or pass forward. 1 or 2 players should apply direct pressure and the other players converge,

block potential passing options and mark other players. This creates a numerical advantage in and around the ball zone.

Once the right back (2) loses the ball, the other 3 defenders all shift across. The left back (3) and one centre back (4) mark their direct opponents and the other centre back (5) moves forward to block off a forward pass and close the space available. The right back (2) and No.8 move to apply direct pressure. No.10 marks the opposing No.10 and the defensive midfielder (6) moves across to block any potential passes inside.

These cohesive movements delay or stop the opposition attacking quickly, allowing time for the team to re-group and get players behind the ball. The red winger (11) can either turn and play a pass back or most likely lose the ball.

138

What is the Tactical Situation?

- Our team start the attack from the back and we have at least 7-8 players in our half.

- There are normally a minimum of 3-4 players (midfielders and forwards) in front of the ball.

- In some cases there will be large distances between the wide players and the central players. This is because teams try to utilise the full width of the pitch when building up play from the back.

- The opposition (if they press us) have many players high up the pitch and in our half.

- Our defenders have a numerical advantage or an equality of numbers.

- Our opponents have a short distance to our goal and will use direct attacks once they win the ball.

- The opponent tries to finish their attack within 6-8 seconds (average).

What Objectives Should We Have?

- To make the transition from attack to defence very quickly, defending well in our own half and limiting the space and time available for our opponents - to prevent them from creating goal scoring opportunities.

- Get as many players back and behind the ball as we can, as soon as possible.

- To create a numerical advantage in and around the ball and our penalty area.

- Players need to position themselves in central areas to guard the 'danger zone' in case the opposition are able to pass into the penalty area.

- To quickly close off the passing channels towards our goal and delay the opposition's attack.

- Prevent the opposition from attacking quickly so that they have to play an extra pass, allowing time to re-group and get players behind the ball.

What Practices/Sessions Can We Create for this Tactical Situation?

- We should set out practices with building up play from the back and basic possession games.

- Defensive organisation and movements in our own half after losing possession.

- Transition to defence games against opponents that press high.

- Defending against opponent's fast attacks, trying to block the channels to our goal. The basic aim of these practices is to get players behind the ball and not concede.

- Press the ball and mark players tightly, with the aim of preventing the opposition scoring within 6-8 seconds, before then trying to recover the ball.

TACTICAL SITUATION 1

JÜRGEN KLOPP TACTICS

Building Up From the Back and Quick Transition to Defence

Analysis taken from Analysis of Liverpool FC during the 2016/2017 Premier League season

The analysis is based on recurring patterns of play observed within the Liverpool team. Once the same phase of play occurred a number of times (at least 10) the tactics would be seen as a pattern. The analysis on the next page is an example of the team's tactics being used effectively, taken from a specific game.

Each action, pass, individual movement with or without the ball, and the positioning of each player on the pitch including their body shape, are presented.

The analysis is then used to create a full progressive session to coach this specific tactical situation.

Analysis Taken from 'Burnley FC vs Liverpool FC - 20 Aug 2016'

Building Up From the Back and Quick Transition to Defence

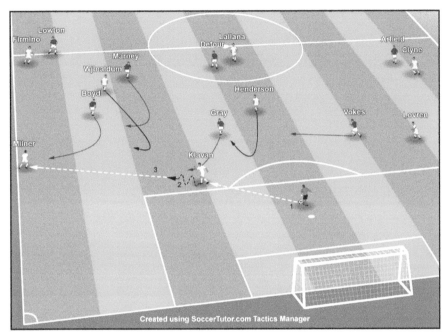

In this example Liverpool start to build up play from the goalkeeper.

The centre back Klavan passes to the left back Milner close to the sideline.

Burnley's right winger Boyd applies pressure in such a way as to block passing options inside and the right back Lowton marks Firmino closely.

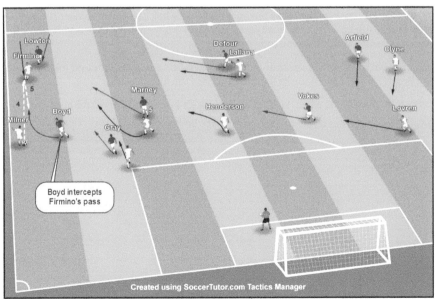

Milner passes to Firmino who is under pressure.

Firmino's pass back is then intercepted by Boyd.

The Liverpool players all shift across to close the space around the ball area.

COACHING TRANSITION PLAY

Klavan (17) puts Gray under pressure and the ball goes out of play for a goal kick

Created using SoccerTutor.com Tactics Manager

Boyd (21) passes to the striker Gray who runs forward with the ball. The Liverpool players' reactions are quick, cohesive and very effective.

The centre back Klavan (17) and the left back Milner apply pressure to the new ball carrier. This prevents Gray from being able to run inside or play the ball into the penalty area. Instead, he is forced out wide and towards the sideline, where the danger can be reduced and subsequently ended.

Firmino and Wijnaldum also track back to close off space and create a numerical advantage around the ball zone. Henderson tracks the run of Boyd (21) and Lovren tracks the striker Vokes's run into the box.

Klavan (17) tracks Gray closely and tackles him, which leads to a goal kick for Liverpool, when it rebounds off Gray's foot and out of play.

1. Passing and Collective Pressing of the Ball Carrier in an Unopposed Practice

Objective: To develop the collective reactions needed in the transition from defence to attack in the low zone.

Description

Using half a pitch, we have all 11 players in a 4-4-2 formation (you can adjust to your team's formation). The practice starts from the goalkeeper and we play out from the back. The players maintain possession of the ball on the ground with a variety of passes, continuously moving to support the player with the ball.

The players wait for the coach's signal. When it comes, whichever player has possession at that moment becomes the opponent and all the other players make a quick transition from attack to defence, to immediately apply pressure and take up the correct positioning for this tactical situation.

The nearest player (or 2) presses the ball carrier, another provides cover and all of the other players shift together to take up the correct defensive positions.

Rule: The players are limited to 2-3 touches when they play forward and 1 touch when they pass backward.

Variation: In the first phase, the players play a pass forward, followed by a pass backward - continually going front to back.

2. Building Up From the Back and Quick Transition to Defence in a 9 v 5 Zonal Practice

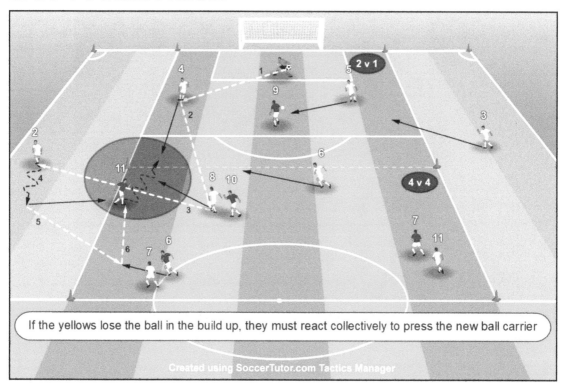

If the yellows lose the ball in the build up, they must react collectively to press the new ball carrier

Description

Using half a pitch again, we mark out 4 zones as shown in the diagram. The yellow team have 9 players including a goalkeeper in a 4-4 formation (or 4-2-2). The red team have 5 players with 1 central midfielder (6), 1 attacking midfielder (10), 2 wingers (7 & 11) and a striker (9). In the low zone we have a 2 v 1 situation between the 2 yellow centre backs (4 & 5) and 1 red striker (9). In the other large zone we have a 4 v 4 situation. We also have 2 yellow full backs (2 & 3) in the side zones.

The practice starts from the goalkeeper and the objective for the yellow team is to build up and keep possession under pressure in their own half, exploiting the numerical advantage at the back and at the sides. When possession is lost, the second objective for the yellow team is to make a quick transition from attack to defence with collective pressing, aiming to stop the reds from scoring, and ultimately recovering the ball.

In the first phase players are restricted to their zones. Once the yellows lose the ball, the zone restrictions are no longer applicable and all players can move freely to defend/attack.

Rules

1. The yellow centre backs (4 & 5) and full backs (2 & 3) are limited to 2 touches and all the other players have unlimited touches.
2. If the yellow team complete 8 consecutive passes, they score 1 point. If the red team win the ball and score a goal, they get 2 points. If the yellows recover the ball within 6 seconds of losing it, they get 1 point.

3. Building Up From the Back and Quick Transition to Defence in a 9 v 6 Game

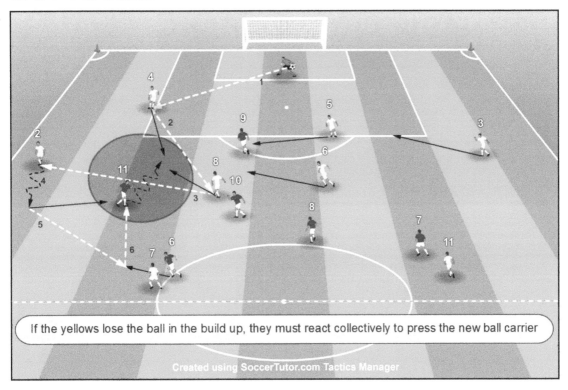

> If the yellows lose the ball in the build up, they must react collectively to press the new ball carrier

Description

In this variation of the previous practice, we remove the zones and play freely in half a pitch. We also add a second central midfielder (8) for the red team.

We now play a 9 v 6 game with the same objectives for both teams as explained in the previous practice.

Rules

1. All players have unlimited touches.
2. If the yellow team complete 8 consecutive passes, they score 1 point.
3. If the yellow team recover the ball within 6 seconds of losing it, they score 1 point.
4. If the red team score a goal they get 2 points.

Variation: Add 2 full backs for the red team. This creates an equality of numbers for the outfield players (8 v 8), which makes it harder for the yellows to keep possession and defend in the transition phase.

Coaching Points

1. Quickly close off the passing channels towards goal and delay the opposition's attack.
2. Prevent the opposition from attacking quickly so they have to play an extra pass, allowing time to re-organise defensively.

PROGRESSION

4. Building Up From the Back and Quick Transition to Defence in an 11 v 11 Game

Created using SoccerTutor.com Tactics Manager

Description

In this progression and final practice of the session, we add a full size goal with a goalkeeper for the red team in the position shown. We play a normal game 11 v 11 game with the yellow team in a 4-4-2 formation and the red team in a 4-2-3-1 formation. You can change these formations to suit your team's training.

The practice starts with the yellow team's goalkeeper and the objective is to build up play from the back and try to score a goal. If the reds win the ball, the second objective for the yellow team is to make a quick transition from attack to defence with collective pressing, trying to stop the reds scoring and recovering the ball.

When an attack finishes or the ball goes out of play, start again with the yellow team's goalkeeper.

Rules

1. All players have unlimited touches.
2. If the yellow team score a goal they get 1 point. If they recover the ball within 6 seconds they get 1 point.
3. The red team must finish their counter attack within 12 seconds of winning the ball.
4. If the red team score a goal within 12 seconds of winning the ball, they get 2 points.

TACTICAL SITUATION 2

PEP GUARDIOLA TACTICS

Condensing the Space in the Centre and
Blocking the Direct Path to Goal

Content taken from Analysis of Manchester City during the 2016/2017 season

The analysis is based on recurring patterns of play observed within the Manchester City team. Once the same phase of play occurred a number of times (at least 10) the tactics would be seen as a pattern. The analysis on the next page is an example of the team's tactics being used effectively, taken from a specific game.

Each action, pass, individual movement with or without the ball, and the positioning of each player on the pitch including their body shape, are presented.

The analysis is then used to create a full progressive session to coach this specific tactical situation.

Analysis Taken from 'Manchester Utd vs Manchester City - 26 Oct 2016 (League Cup)'

Condensing the Space in the Centre and Blocking the Direct
Path to Goal

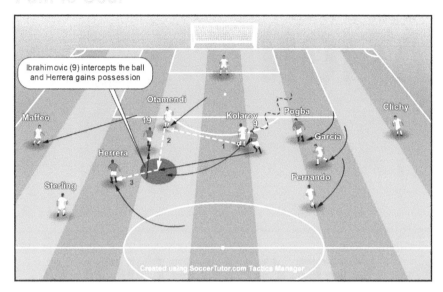

Ibrahimovic (9) intercepts the ball
and Herrera gains possession

In this situation, Man City are building up play from the back.

Kolarov carries the ball forward and is put under pressure by Ibrahimovic (9). Kolarov then turns back and passes to the centre back Otamendi.

Otamendi then tries to pass to Kolarov who has made a forward run. Ibrahimovic (9) gets to the ball first and intercepts. Herrera ends up with the ball.

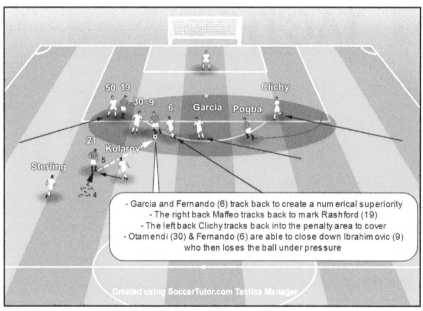

- Garcia and Fernando (6) track back to create a numerical superiority
- The right back Maffeo tracks back to mark Rashford (19)
- The left back Clichy tracks back into the penalty area to cover
- Otamendi (30) & Fernando (6) are able to close down Ibrahimovic (9) who then loses the ball under pressure

Herrera carries the ball forward and is under pressure from Kolarov. He passes inside to Ibrahimovic (9).

The Man City players all move into the centre to condense the space. Otamendi (30) and Fernando (6) are able to close down Ibrahimovic (9) who has no passing options and loses the ball under pressure.

With this collective movement to condense the space in the centre, Man City are able to block the direct path to goal through the centre, which is the most dangerous scenario when losing possession in the low zone.

1. Condensing the Space in the Centre After Losing Possession in a 5 v 5 (+2) Transition Game

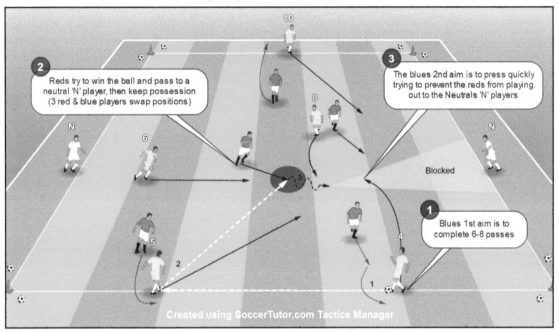

2 Reds try to win the ball and pass to a neutral 'N' player, then keep possession (3 red & blue players swap positions)

3 The blues 2nd aim is to press quickly trying to prevent the reds from playing out to the Neutrals 'N' players

Blocked

1 Blues 1st aim is to complete 6-8 passes

Created using SoccerTutor.com Tactics Manager

Objective: To work on collective pressing in the transition from attack to defence - to condense the space in the centre and prevent the opposition from playing out.

Description

In a 25 x 25 yard area we play 5 v 5 with 2 additional neutral players (yellow) who always play with the team in possession.

One team starts in possession (blues in diagram example) and they have 2 players outside at the bottom of the area (centre backs - 4 & 5), 2 players inside the area (central midfielders - 6 & 8) and 1 player outside at the top (attacking midfielder - 10). The neutral players are positioned outside on the sides. The other team (reds) have all of their 5 players inside the area.

The objectives are:

1. The first objective for the blue team (with help from the neutrals) is to complete 6-8 consecutive passes to score 1 point.

2. The red team apply collective pressing to try and win the ball. If the blues lose possession, the 3 outside blue players and 3 red inside players swap positions. The team roles are reversed.

3. The blue team's second objective is to then try to recover the ball as soon as possible. They need to be quick and press with the correct angles to block passes to the outside neutral players, as shown.

The teams learn the rhythm of trying to keep possession, losing the ball and then trying to win the ball back as quickly as possible. If the ball goes out of play, start again with the same team in possession.

149

VARIATION

2. Condensing the Space in the Centre After Losing Possession in a 7 v 5 Transition Game

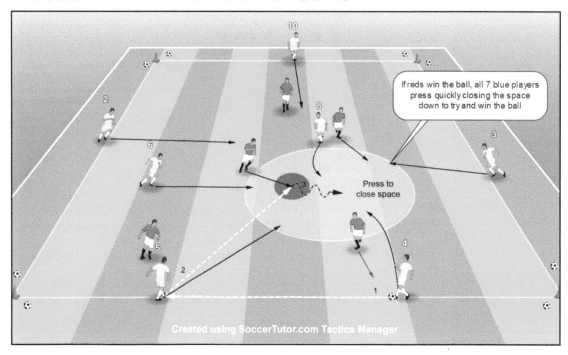

If reds win the ball, all 7 blue players press quickly closing the space down to try and win the ball

Press to close space

Created using SoccerTutor.com Tactics Manager

Objective: To work on collective pressing in the transition from attack to defence - to condense the space in the centre and recover the ball as soon as possible.

Description

In this variation of the previous practice, we replace the 2 neutral players at the sides with 2 blue players who act as full backs (2 & 3).

We now have a 7 v 5 situation with the exact same objectives as the previous practice, but now all 5 red players stay inside the area if they win the ball. When the blue team lose the ball, all 7 blue players apply immediate pressure to get the ball back again from the 5 red players.

Rules

1. If the blue team complete 6-8 consecutive passes in the first phase, they score 1 point.
2. If the red team keep the ball for 6-8 seconds, they score 1 point.
3. If the red team complete 6 consecutive passes, they score 2 points.
4. If the blue team recover the ball within 6 seconds they score 1 point.

Coaching Point

When the blues have the ball, they should *OPEN* the pitch (making the area as big as possible to keep possession) and when they lose the ball, they should *CLOSE* it (denying space and time for the opposition).

3. Condensing the Space in the Centre After Losing Possession in a 7 v 5 Transition Game with 4 Goals

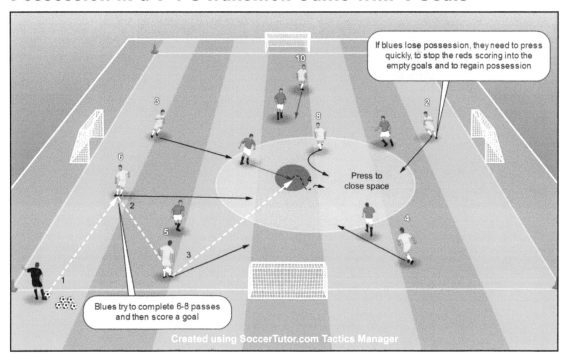

Description

In this progression of the previous practice, all 12 players now play inside the same 25 x 25 yard area and we have 1 small goal on each side as shown (4 total).

The practice starts with the coach's pass and the 7 blue players are in possession. Their objective is to complete 6-8 passes and then try to score in one of the 4 goals (1 point).

The red players press the blue team and try to win the ball before 6-8 passes are completed. If the blues lose the ball, their second objective is to condense the space in the centre and block any potential passing options.

Rules

1. If the blue team complete 6-8 passes and then score a goal in the first phase, they get 1 point.
2. If the red team manage to win the ball and keep it for 6 seconds they score 1 point.
3. If the red team score a goal they get 2 points.
4. If the blue team recover the ball within 6 seconds, they score 1 point. If they then score they get 1 more point.

Coaching Points

1. By implementing the rules above, we force the 7 blue players to make a very quick transition from attack to defence, to prevent their opponents from scoring any points. This adds a competitive edge which increases the intensity of the practice.
2. The empty goals force quick reactions as it is easy for the opposition to score if they are given any free space.

151

PROGRESSION

4. Condensing the Space in the Centre and Forcing the Play Wide in a 6 (+2) v 6 (+2) SSG

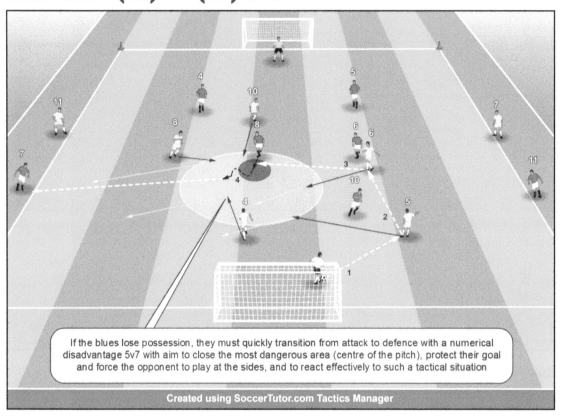

If the blues lose possession, they must quickly transition from attack to defence with a numerical disadvantage 5v7 with aim to close the most dangerous area (centre of the pitch), protect their goal and force the opponent to play at the sides, and to react effectively to such a tactical situation

Created using SoccerTutor.com Tactics Manager

Description

In a 35 x 35 yard area we have 2 full size goals and 2 teams of 8 players. Inside the area we have a 5 v 5 situation with both teams in a 2-2-1 formation. Both teams also have 2 wingers positioned outside at the sides (7 & 11).

We start with a keeper and play a normal 5 v 5 game. When a team loses the ball (blues), their aim is to condense the space in the centre and block the direct path to goal (forcing play wide). The team in transition from defence to attack (reds) have a numerical advantage as they can use both of their wide players for a 7 v 5 attack.

When possession is lost, all 5 blue players move quickly to close the space in the centre, block off passing options towards goal and force the play wide. If the ball is played wide (e.g. to No.7 in diagram), the blues must react collectively again to the new tactical situation. When an attack finishes, the practice always starts with the goalkeeper from the team that just finished their attack.

Different Rules

1. In the transition from defence to attack, the team must finish their attack within 8-12 seconds.

2. If the team in transition from attack to defence recover the ball within 6 seconds, they score 1 point.

3. The 2 outside players can both go inside the area for a transition to attack. You decide if they can score or not.

PROGRESSION

5. Condensing the Space in the Centre and Forcing the Play Wide in a Tactical Game with Side Zones

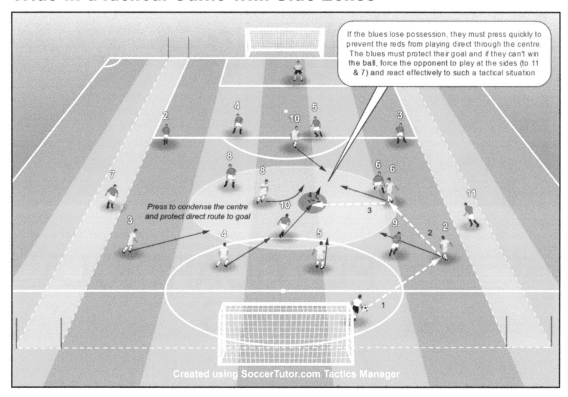

If the blues lose possession, they must press quickly to prevent the reds from playing direct through the centre. The blues must protect their goal and if they can't win the ball, force the opponent to play at the sides (to 11 & 7) and react effectively to such a tactical situation

Press to condense the centre and protect direct route to goal

Created using SoccerTutor.com Tactics Manager

Description

In this progression of the previous practice, we increase the size of the area and add 2 blue full backs (2 & 3), 2 red full backs (2 & 3) and a red striker (9). The 2 red wingers (7 & 11) are positioned in the side zones, with all the other players in the main zone. The blue team are in a 4-2-1 formation and the red team are in a 4-2-3-1 formation.

The practice always starts with the blue team's goalkeeper. The objectives and rules are exactly the same for both teams as they were in the previous practice, but now we have a numerical disadvantage of 7 v 10 for the blue team if the reds win the ball. They must make a quick transition from attack to defence.

It is extremely important to quickly condense the space in the centre and block the direct path to goal (forcing the play out wide into the side zones). If the reds successfully pass the ball into a side zone, the blues must react collectively again to the new tactical situation, shift across collectively to defend and try to recover the ball.

The red wingers (7 & 11) must stay within the side zones but they are limited to 2 or 3 touches.

Coaching Points

1. Quickly close off the passing channels towards goal and stop the ball carrier from dribbling forward. Condense the space in the centre to force the play away from goal and try to recover the ball.
2. Press collectively and quickly stop the reds from attacking quickly, forcing them to play backwards or wide.

TACTICAL SITUATION 3

PEP GUARDIOLA TACTICS

Quick Transition to Defend inside the Penalty Area

Content taken from Analysis of Manchester City during the 2016/2017 Champions League Group Stage

The analysis is based on recurring patterns of play observed within the Manchester City team. Once the same phase of play occurred a number of times (at least 10) the tactics would be seen as a pattern. The analysis on the next page is an example of the team's tactics being used effectively, taken from a specific game.

Each action, pass, individual movement with or without the ball, and the positioning of each player on the pitch including their body shape, are presented.

The analysis is then used to create a full progressive session to coach this specific tactical situation.

Analysis Taken from 'Manchester City vs FC Barcelona - 1 Nov 2016'

Quick Transition to Defend Inside the Penalty Area

In this situation Man City are building up play from the goalkeeper.

The centre back Otamendi receives and carries the ball forward. He is closed down by Neymar and passes forward to Sterling (7).

Sterling (7) takes a bad touch and the ball is intercepted by Busquets (5). Busquets (5) passes to Rakitic, who passes to Suarez (9).

Man City now need to make a quick transition from attack to defence.

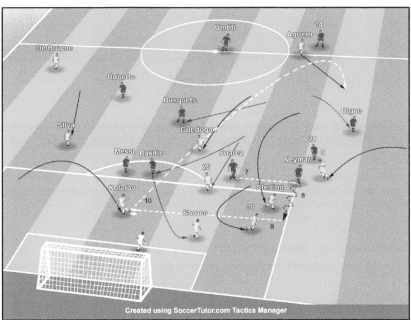

Suarez passes to Neymar. Zabaleta (5), Sterling (7) and Otamendi (30) all move quickly to close down the new ball carrier (Neymar) who dribbles forward with the ball. The other Man City players quickly track back, with 5 players in total defending inside the penalty area.

Neymar attempts a low cross - Kolarov has moved across and clears the ball towards Aguero.

This is an example of a successful transition from attack to defence for Pep Guardiola's Man City.

SESSION FOR THIS TACTICAL SITUATION (4 PRACTICES)

1. Quick Transition to Defend in 1 v 1 Duels with Support Players

1/2

Go !

C

L

R

1 — Players begin by passing back and forth

2 — On the coach's signal, the player with the ball becomes attacker for 1 v 1 duel

R

L

R

L

Created using SoccerTutor.com Tactics Manager

Objective: Developing the transition from attack to defence in 1 v 1 situations close to goal.

Description

In a 20 x 40 yard area we have 2 full size goals with goalkeepers. There are 2 teams with 3 players each. Inside the area there are 2 players in a 1 v 1 situation and the other 4 players (2 on each team) are outside at the sides with balls, as shown in the diagram.

The practice starts with the 2 inside players passing the ball to each other until the coach gives his signal. When the coach calls out, the player who has the ball becomes the attacker (blue player in diagram example) and the other player (red) becomes the defender in a 1 v 1 duel.

Rules

1. When the players are passing the ball to each other at the beginning they are limited to 1 touch.
2. In the first 1 v 1 (phase 1 shown in diagram above), the players have unlimited touches.

The description of phase 2 is on the next page...

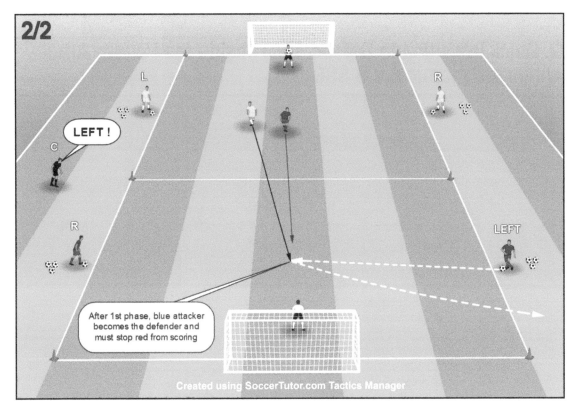

When the first phase of attack finishes, the roles of the players change - the attacker (blue) becomes the defender and the defender (red) becomes the attacker.

As soon as the first phase is finished, the coach calls out 'Left' or 'Right' which determines which outside player in the other half is going to cross a new ball into play.

Both players run quickly towards the other goal for a new 1 v 1 battle, fighting for the ball that is crossed by the outside player. In this example, the red player is trying to score and the blue player defends the goal. The blue defender is able to get to the ball first and kick the ball out of play.

Rule: In this second 1 v 1 (shown in diagram above), the players are limited to 2 touches.

PROGRESSION

2. Quick Transition to Defend 1 v 1 inside the Penalty Area within a Dynamic 8 v 8 SSG

As soon as attack finishes, the coach calls out number of 2 players who must contest a 1v1 in the box & which side the cross is delivered from. The defender is from the team that just finished their attack (blue No.4).

Created using SoccerTutor.com Tactics Manager

Description

Using half a pitch we create a playing zone approximately 35 x 55 yards. We have 2 full size goals and play a normal 8 v 8 game within the zone. The teams can use the same or different formations and all players are numbered (1 to 7). We also have a goal and a goalkeeper in the normal position with 2 players (yellow) near the sidelines, ready to cross balls into the penalty area.

The practice starts with one of the team's goalkeeper (blue in diagram) and we play a normal 8 v 8 game. When one team finishes an attack, the coach calls out a number and a side (e.g. '4 - Right'). The 2 players who have their numbers called out then quickly run into the penalty area for a 1 v 1 duel.

The cross is delivered from the side that the coach calls out (left or right). The player from the team that just finished their attack makes a transition from attack to defence (blue No.4 in diagram), trying to prevent the opponent from scoring. The opposing No.4 (red) tries to score.

Once the 1 v 1 is finished, the practice starts again in the main zone from the red team's goalkeeper, with the team roles and objectives reversed.

Coaching Points

1. The player in transition from attack to defence needs to have quick reactions and make sure to get into position inside the penalty area before the opposing attacker.
2. The defender should get goal side of the attacker and side-on to the ball, before making a clearance.

3. Press, Win the Ball, Switch the Point of Defence and Quick Transition to Defend inside the Penalty Area

Scenario 1: When the red team start in possession

If the blues win ball, the coach calls out a number of a red outside player who then starts a new attack.

Created using SoccerTutor.com Tactics Manager

Description

In this progression of the previous practice, we now use the full width of the pitch and create a zone from the edge of the penalty area to the halfway line and mark out 3 small goals with large cones as shown in the diagram.

Within the main zone we have a 6 v 6 situation with the blue team in a 4-2 formation against the red team who are in a 4-1-1 or 2-3-1 formation. The red team also have 3 extra players (numbered randomly 1-3) with a ball in the 3 small cone goals on the halfway line.

The practice starts with the red team in possession trying to create chances and score a goal. If the blue team win the ball, the coach then calls out a number and that outside red player (1, 2 or 3) immediately runs into the zone with a new ball. The red team then have 12-14 seconds to finish their attack.

After winning the ball in the first phase, the blue team must then change immediately back to defending again. They must defend their goal with a numerical disadvantage (6 v 7).

*If the blue team are able stop the attack or win the ball in the second phase, the coach calls out which yellow player will cross the ball (right or left). At this point, all of the players are allowed to enter the penalty area. The reds attack and try to score. The blues are again in a transition from attack to defence and try to defend their goal - **See Page 161**.*

Scenario 2: When the blue team start in possession

If the blues score in one of the small cone goals, the coach calls out the number of a red outside player who then starts a new attack. The blues must change immediately back to defending again.

Created using SoccerTutor.com Tactics Manager

Description

In this second scenario, it is the blue team that now start in possession.

The practice starts with the blue team's goalkeeper who passes to one of the defenders, as shown in the diagram. The blue team build up play and try to find solutions to score in one of the 3 small cone goals on the halfway line (1 point).

If the blue team score or the attack finishes, then the coach calls out a number and that outside red player (1, 2 or 3) immediately runs into the zone with a new ball. In this example it is red No.3 and the red team then have 12-14 seconds to finish their attack.

After scoring or finishing their attack in the first phase, the blue team must then change immediately back to defending again. As a new player and ball enter the pitch, they must defend their goal with a numerical disadvantage (6 v 7).

The description of scenario 2 continues with the diagram on the next page...

LEFT! 8a

> If the blues win the ball back again, the coach calls out 'LEFT' or 'RIGHT' and that player crosses a ball into the box for the reds to attack. The blues must change immediately back to defending again, this time in the penalty area.

Created using SoccerTutor.com Tactics Manager

This diagram is a continuation of scenario 2. The red outside player(No.3) has dribbled into play to start a new attack.

If the blue team are able to stop the attack or win the ball in this second phase, the coach calls out which yellow player will cross the ball (right or left). At this point, all of the players are allowed to enter the penalty area. The reds attack and try to score. The blues are in a transition from attack to defence again and try to defend the goal.

Rules (for Scenarios 1 & 2)

1. All players have unlimited touches.
2. As soon as an outside red player enters with a ball, the red team have 12-14 seconds to finish their attack.
3. As soon as the coach calls out which yellow player is to cross (right or left), the red team have 6 seconds to finish their attack.
4. If the red team score a goal they get 1 point.
5. If the blue team stop an attack or win the ball they get 1 point.
6. If the blue team score in one of the 3 small cone goals on the halfway line (scenario 2), they get 2 points.

Coaching Points

1. There needs to be good defensive organisation and movements in our own half after losing possession. Limit the space and time available for the opposition - prevent them from creating goal scoring opportunities.
2. Players need to position themselves in central areas to guard the 'danger zone' in case the opposition are able to pass into the penalty area.
3. Press the ball and mark tightly - prevent the opposition scoring within 8 seconds, then try to recover the ball.

4. Quick Transition to Defend inside the Penalty Area in a Dynamic 8 v 8 SSG

Description

In this variation of the previous practice, we extend the size of the large zone up to the penalty spot and replace the 3 mini goals with a full size goal and goalkeeper.

We have an 8 v 8 situation in the large zone with the outfield players. Each team also has a goalkeeper and the red team have another 2 players (yellows) near the sidelines, ready to cross balls in. The teams can use the same or different formations.

We start with the blue team's goalkeeper and the blues build up play and try to score a goal. When the blue team finish an attack, the coach calls out a side (left or right). At this point, 3 players from each team quickly run into the final zone to contest an incoming cross.

The cross is delivered from the side that the coach calls out (left in diagram example). The players from the team that just finished their attack (blues) make a transition from attack to defence, trying to prevent the 3 red players from scoring.

If the red team score or the ball goes out of play, the practice starts again from the blue team's goalkeeper. If the blues intercept the ball, the game carries on as normal.

Progression: An unlimited amount of players from both teams can make runs to attack/defend the cross.

CHAPTER 9

TRANSITION FROM ATTACK TO DEFENCE IN THE MIDDLE ZONE

TRANSITION FROM ATTACK TO DEFENCE IN THE MIDDLE ZONE

The red centre back (4) wins the ball from the No.10 so the white team make a transition from attack to defence

MIDDLE ZONE

Created using SoccerTutor.com Tactics Manager

For this book, we have divided the chapters by which zone the transition starts in. There are 3 zones:

1. **Low Zone**
2. Middle Zone
3. **High Zone**

This diagram shows an example of a team losing the ball in the middle zone. In this situation, the red team's centre back (4) wins the ball from the white No.10. There are players behind the ball and many players concentrated in the centre of the pitch (both teams).

It is again important that pressure is applied to the new ball carrier immediately, before he is able to get his head up to dribble or pass forward. The white team's defensive midfielder (6) closes down the ball carrier immediately and also blocks the pass to

No.9. The left back (3), the right back (2), the central midfielder (8) and both wingers (11 & 7) all track back to mark a red player and prevent the ball being played to them.

When losing the ball in the middle zone, there is often free space in behind the defensive line. This is why the cohesive movements are so important. As shown in the diagram, all of the players move into the central area. This closes the space in which the opposition can play and prevents them from playing the ball wide or utilising the space in behind.

The players need to work together as a full team, because if just one player doesn't react quickly enough, the opposition could have an easy passing opportunity in behind with a goal scoring chance. If it is done effectively, the team will recover possession.

What is the Tactical Situation?

- Our team have the ball approximately the same distance from our goal as they do to the opponent's goal.

- We have free space in behind our defensive line and there are many players concentrated in the centre of the pitch from both teams.

- The opposition will have many different attacking solutions if we lose the ball. They have the possibility to attack with 5-6 players and make runs in behind our defensive line.

- The opposition forwards can provide support easily and at least 2-3 players can move forward from midfield.

- We are often unorganised when we lose the ball in the middle zone. The positions that we have when losing the ball in this area sometimes make the reactions slow and ineffective.

- The negative transitions can be with an equality of numbers or we may face a numerical disadvantage.

- The opposition's counter attack takes 8 seconds on average.

What Objectives Should We Have?

- To maintain good positions when we have possession in the middle zone, so we can react quickly and efficiently when we lose the ball, thus reducing the risk.

- To quickly pass from attack to defence, trying to deny the opposition time and space - making sure to prevent passes being played in behind our defensive line.

- There should be an immediate press of the opponent's new ball carrier from our nearest player. There also needs to be fast tracking back and support from other teammates to create a strong side with a numerical advantage near the ball zone.

- The players in the centre of the pitch (centre backs, central midfielders) must be able to read the tactical situation and provide defensive balance. If there is an open ball situation, they should look to prevent the opposition from exploiting space in behind, They move back together and track the runs of the opposition players.

What Practices/Sessions Can We Create for this Tactical Situation?

- Possession situations in the middle zone versus opponents trying to defend in there and win the ball. We practice situations that lead to quick transitions from attack to defence in all possible scenarios.

- We work on fast reactions when we lose the ball in any tactical situations, anywhere in the middle zone. There should be a focus on synchronised defensive movements from our team - this depends on our formation and the strengths and weaknesses of the opposition and their formation.

TACTICAL SITUATION 1

JÜRGEN KLOPP TACTICS

Quick Transition to Defence in the Middle Zone

Analysis taken from 'Jürgen Klopp's Defending Tactics' (Athanasios Terzis 2015)

Available to buy from SoccerTutor.com (paperback + eBook)

The analysis is based on recurring patterns of play. Once the same phase of play occurred a number of times (at least 10) the tactics would be decoded, with the positioning of each player on the pitch studied in great detail, including their body shape. Each individual movement with or without the ball was also recorded in detail. The analysis on the next page is an example of the team's tactics being used effectively.

The analysis is then used to create a full progressive session to coach this specific tactical situation.

Analysis taken from 'Jürgen Klopp's Defending Tactics' (Athanasios Terzis)
Quick Transition to Defence in the Middle Zone

No.5 wins the ball from Blaszczykowski (16) and passes forward to No.6

In this example, the Borussia Dortmund winger Blaszczykowski (16) had possession and ran inside, with the right back Piszczek (26) having made an overlapping run.

The red centre back (5) wins the ball from Blaszczykowski (16) and passes to No.6. Bender (6) puts pressure on him and Mkhitaryan (10) moves to help double mark him.

Piszczek (26) drops back immediately and Sahin (18) marks the red No.10 closely.

Klopp's Borussia Dortmund team would look to apply immediate pressure on the new ball carrier when possession was lost in the middle zone. This would create a numerical advantage around the ball zone and often lead to Dortmund recovering the ball very quickly.

SESSION FOR THIS TACTICAL SITUATION (5 PRACTICES)
1. Dynamic 6 v 6 (+6) Small Sided Game with 6 Mini Goals

If yellows lose the ball, they make a fast transition to defence

Yellows build up & try to score

Created using SoccerTutor.com Tactics Manager

Objective: To develop continuous transitions from attack to defence and to block the quick forward passes and direct game from the opposition.

Description

In a 40 x 40 yard area we have 3 mini goals at each end and 3 teams with 6 players each. One team plays the role of neutral support players in the positions shown in the diagram (blues) - they always play with the team in possession.

We play a normal 6 (+6) v 6 game with the aim to circulate the ball quickly forward and try to score in one of the 3 mini goals. The game starts with a neutral player passing to one team (yellows in diagram) who then attack. They need to make sure to utilise the neutral outside players as much as possible, to exploit their numerical advantage.

When a team loses the ball, they need to make a very quick transition from attack to defence. This is because the team that won the ball has a numerical advantage (with use of the neutral players) for their fast break attack and can score in 3 goals.

Rules

1. The players are limited to 2 or 3 touches and the outside neutral players are limited to 1 or 2 touches.
2. Each goal scores 1 point but if a team is able to complete 8 consecutive passes before scoring, they get 2 points.
3. If a team recovers the ball within 6 seconds of losing it, they score 1 point.

COACHING TRANSITION PLAY

2. Dynamic Four Team Transition Game Across Two Parallel Grids

> When the ball goes out of play, the coach calls out which players should swap pitches

> YELLOW 2

Created using SoccerTutor.com Tactics Manager

Objective: To develop the transition from attack to defence with constant changes in the game situation.

Description

In this progression we have 2 parallel pitches (18 x 28 yards each) with full size goals and goalkeepers. We have 4 teams with 6 players each.

2 teams take up the same outside neutral positions as used in the last practice (blues and oranges in diagram example). The other 2 teams (reds and yellows) split their players so that they have 3 players in each grid. This creates 2 games with a 3 (+6) v 3 situation.

We number the inside players (1-3) and play a normal game starting from the goalkeeper, with the objective to score a goal (1 point). As soon as the ball goes out of play in either game, the coach calls out for 2 players to switch grids e.g. 'Yellow 2' or 'Red 3'. These 2 players must then run across to the other grid, recognise the situation and quickly adapt to the new position they need to take up, respective of their teammates.

Change the team roles often so that the players receive sufficient rest during their role as neutral support players.

Variation: The coach can call out 2 numbers. Alternatively the coach can call out a colour (e.g. red or yellow), so all 6 players on that team (3 from each grids) must then switch. This forces the whole team to make a very quick transition and get across in time to prevent the opposition from scoring.

PROGRESSION

3. Build Up Play and Transition to Defence in a Position Specific Game with Target Players

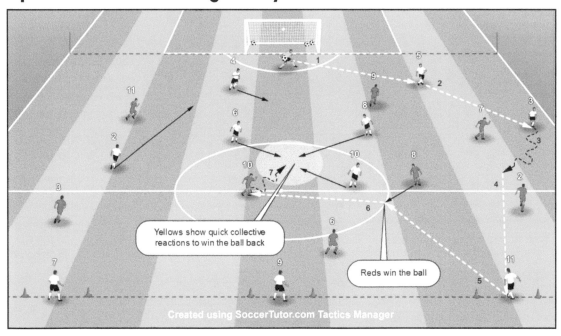

Yellows show quick collective reactions to win the ball back

Reds win the ball

Created using SoccerTutor.com Tactics Manager

Objective: To develop possession and quick forward passing from the back + transition from attack to defence.

Description

We mark out an area from the edge of the penalty area (full size goal with goalkeeper) to 20 yards past the halfway line (3 mini cone goals) as shown in the diagram. Both teams have 7 players within the area. The yellow team are in a 4-2-1 formation and the red team are in a 2-3-3 formation (from 4-3-3 with 2 full backs). There are an additional 3 yellow target players (7, 9 & 11) positioned inside the small cone goals and they play as support players.

The practice starts from the yellow goalkeeper and the aim is to build up play from the back, trying to move the ball forward quickly to score as soon as possible. To score, a yellow player has to pass to a teammate inside one of the small goals. They then play the ball back inside to a teammate and the practice continues with the same aim.

The objective for the red team is to apply pressure, win the ball and then launch a fast break attack to score. If this is achieved, the yellow team must move very quickly from attack to defence, stop the reds from scoring and recover the ball. The movements of the yellow team to try and recover possession are shown in the diagram.

Rules

1. The yellow players are limited to 3 touches and the target players are limited to 1 touch. The red players have unlimited touches, but they have a limited time to finish their fast break attack (e.g. 8-10 seconds).
2. The yellow target players are not allowed to pass to each other.
3. You can decide whether the target players can enter the pitch to assist in the negative transition.

4. Build Up Play and Transition to Defence in a Position Specific Game

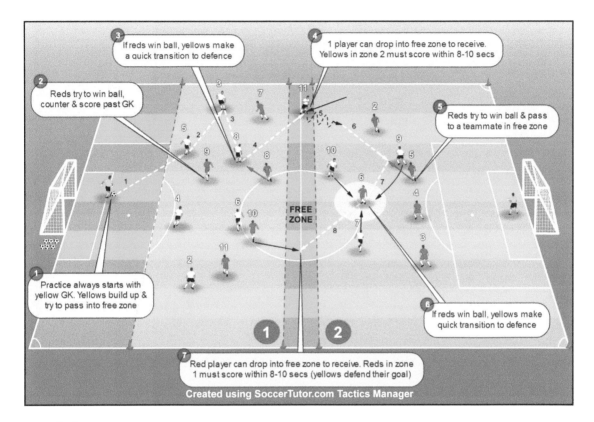

3 If reds win ball, yellows make a quick transition to defence

4 1 player can drop into free zone to receive. Yellows in zone 2 must score within 8-10 secs

2 Reds try to win ball, counter & score past GK

5 Reds try to win ball & pass to a teammate in free zone

1 Practice always starts with yellow GK. Yellows build up & try to pass into free zone

6 If reds win ball, yellows make quick transition to defence

7 Red player can drop into free zone to receive. Reds in zone 1 must score within 8-10 secs (yellows defend their goal)

Created using SoccerTutor.com Tactics Manager

Description

We use a full pitch and mark out 2 zones as shown in the diagram. In zone 1 we have 6 yellow players in a 4-2 formation (from 4-2-3-1) and 5 red players in a 2-3 formation (from 4-3-3). In zone 2 we have 4 yellow players in a 3-1 formation (from 4-2-3-1) and 5 red players in a 4-1 formation (from 4-3-3).

The practice always starts with the yellow team's goalkeeper who passes into zone 1. The yellows build up and aim to pass into the free zone for a teammate from zone 2. If the reds win the ball in zone 1 they must score past the goalkeeper within 8-10 seconds. The yellows make a quick transition to defence to try and recover the ball.

One yellow player (No.11 in diagram) can drop into the free zone and receive. The yellows must then score past the red goalkeeper within 8-10 seconds. If they don't or the ball goes out of play, the practice starts again from the yellow team's goalkeeper.

The reds try to win the ball and then pass into the free zone. The yellows make a quick transition to defence and aim to recover the ball. One red player (No.10 in diagram) can drop into the free zone and receive. The reds must then score past the goalkeeper within 8-10 seconds. If they don't or the ball goes out of play, the practice starts again from the yellow team's goalkeeper.

All players have unlimited touches throughout the entire practice.

171

PROGRESSION

5. Intense 11 v 11 Transition Play Within the Middle Zone

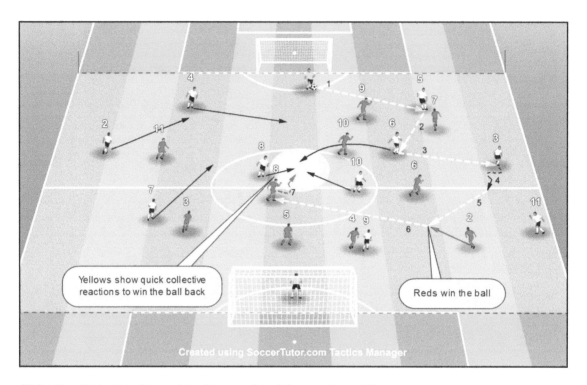

Yellows show quick collective reactions to win the ball back

Reds win the ball

Created using SoccerTutor.com Tactics Manager

Objective: To develop the transition from attack to defence in the middle zone.

Description

In the final practice of this session we use the area in between the 2 penalty boxes and play an 11 v 11 game. The yellow team are in a 4-2-3-1 formation and the red team are in a 4-3-3 formation.

The practice always starts with a goalkeeper and that team build up from the back with the aim to score a goal. The other team (reds in diagram) must focus on defending collectively, pressing and trying to win the ball. After winning the ball, they then launch a fast break attack to try and score.

The second objective for the team that started with possession (yellows) is to make a quick and effective transition from attack to defence, preventing their opponents from scoring and trying to win the ball back as soon as possible. The movements of the yellow team to try and recover possession are shown in the diagram.

Key Point: The confined space of the pitch forces the teams to lose the ball in the middle zone more frequently than usual, so the players get to practice the transition from attack to defence in this area more often, which is the element we are working on improving.

TACTICAL SITUATION 2

JÜRGEN KLOPP TACTICS

Defensive Reactions to an Open Ball Situation

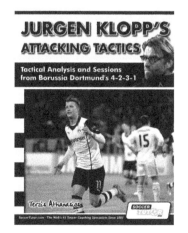

Analysis taken from 'Jürgen Klopp's Attacking Tactics'
(Athanasios Terzis 2015)

Available to buy from SoccerTutor.com (paperback + eBook)

The analysis is based on recurring patterns of play. Once the same phase of play occurred a number of times (at least 10) the tactics would be decoded, with the positioning of each player on the pitch studied in great detail, including their body shape. Each individual movement with or without the ball was also recorded in detail. The analysis on the next page is an example of the team's tactics being used effectively.

The analysis is then used to create a full progressive session to coach this specific tactical situation.

Analysis taken from 'Jürgen Klopp's Defending Tactics' (Athanasios Terzis)
Defensive Reactions to an Open Ball Situation

Blaszczykowski (16) loses the ball to No.5 and the opposition have time and space

In this example, we see what happens when Klopp's Borussia Dortmund team were unable to win the ball back immediately after losing it. They had to use collective movement to retain the team shape and defend the paths to their goal.

Red No.5 wins the ball from Blaszczykowski (16) and passes to No.11 who has space in front of him before Bender (6) is able to close him down. As there is an open ball situation, the red forwards make forward runs and the Dortmund defenders drop back to prevent a pass in behind the defensive line.

The aim for the defensive midfielder Bender (6) is to close down No.11 without going to ground, giving time to the right back Piszczek (26) to drop back into an effective defensive position.

Mkhitaryan (10) also drops back and provides balance in midfield.

SESSION FOR THIS TACTICAL SITUATION (4 PRACTICES)
1. Defensive Reactions After Finishing an Attack in a Dynamic 7 v 7 Transition Game

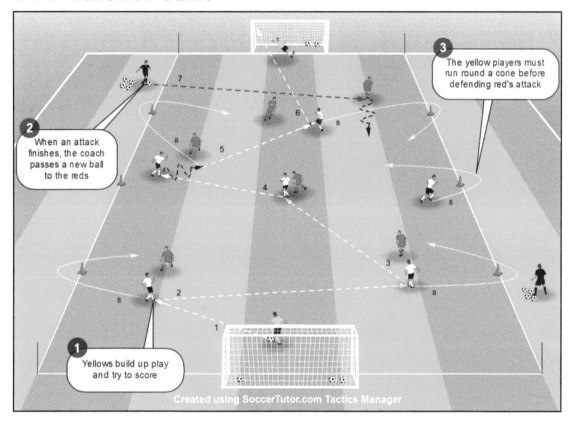

Objective: To work on quick reactions during the transition to defence after finishing an attack.

Description

In a 20 x 40 yard area we have 2 full size goals with goalkeepers and 6 large cones along the sidelines (3 on each side), as shown in the diagram. We play a normal 7 v 7 game starting with one of the goalkeepers.

When a team finishes an attack (or the coach signals), all the players from that team (yellows in diagram example) must run very quickly round one of the large cones. The coach or goalkeeper passes a new ball into the red team as they attack and try to score, so the yellow players must quickly get back inside for the transition from attack to defence. The white arrows show the movements around the cones after the attack finishes or a signal is given.

Rules

1. All players have unlimited touches.
2. The team in transition from defence to attack (reds) have a limited time to finish their attack e.g. 8 seconds.
3. A goal in the first phase scores 1 point and a goal in the transition from defence to attack scores 2 points.
4. If the team in transition from attack to defence stop their opponent's counter attack and recover the ball, they score 1 point.

175

VARIATION

2. Defensive Reactions After Finishing an Attack in a 5 (+4) v 5 (+4) Transition Game

When attack finishes, yellow inside/outside players must swap positions before defending red's attack

Yellows build up play and try to score

Created using SoccerTutor.com Tactics Manager

Description

In this variation of the previous practice, we now play a 5 v 5 game inside the same 20 x 40 yard area. Each team has 4 additional players outside of the area in their opponent's half, as shown in the diagram.

The practice starts with one of the team's goalkeepers (yellows in diagram) and that team try to build up play and score. If and when the yellows finish their attack, the 4 yellow inside players must switch positions with the 4 yellow outside players.

The red goalkeeper plays the ball out if he makes a save or passes a new ball to the red team if a goal is scored, or if the ball goes out of play. The reds then launch a fast break attack and try to score before the yellows can get organised. The 4 new yellow players must quickly get back to defend and try to recover the ball.

Rules

1. All players have unlimited touches.
2. The team in transition from defence to attack (reds) have a limited time to finish their attack e.g. 8 seconds.
3. A goal in the first phase scores 1 point and a goal in the transition from defence to attack scores 2 points.
4. If the team in transition from attack to defence stop their opponents and recover the ball, they score 1 point.

176

3. Team Shape and Reactions to the Transition from Attack to Defence in an 11 v 11 Game (1)

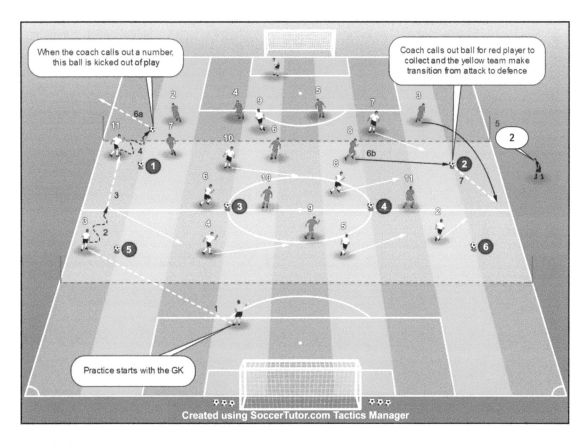

Description

In this practice we mark out a middle zone and play 11 v 11. Inside the zone we have 6 balls (numbered 1-6) in the different positions shown in the diagram. The yellow team are in a 4-2-3-1 formation and the red team are in a 4-3-3 formation - you can adjust these to any formations that suit your team's training.

The practice starts with the yellow team's goalkeeper and a 7th ball as the yellow team build up play and attack the opposition's goal. The coach can call out a number at any time - the current ball should be kicked out of play and the game continues with the new ball called out by the coach.

This game forces the team in possession (yellows) to make a very quick transition from attack to defence and face a new tactical situation in another area of the pitch. Players have to adapt very quickly and efficiently as a team.

Rules

1. The ball has to be collected by the team who were defending when the coach calls out the ball number (reds). You can progress to letting both teams compete for the ball (first to ball wins possession for his team).
2. A goal in the first phase scores 1 point. A goal in the transition from defence to attack scores 2 points.
3. Recovering the ball in the transition from attack to defence scores 1 point.

VARIATION

4. Team Shape and Reactions to the Transition from Attack to Defence in an 11 v 11 Game (2)

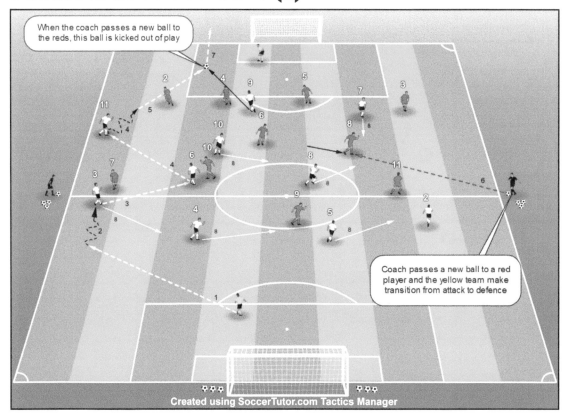

Description

In this variation of the previous practice, we remove the 6 numbered balls and the middle zone.

The yellow team are still in a 4-2-3-1 formation and the red team are in a 4-3-3 formation - you can adjust these to any formations that suit your team's training.

Instead of the coach calling out a number, he can now pass a new ball to the defending team at any time (the team that were in possession kick their ball out of play).

This again forces the team to make a very quick transition from attack to defence and face a new tactical situation in another area of the pitch. Players have to adapt very quickly and efficiently as a team (collectively).

Rules

1. The coach always passes the new ball to a player on the team who were defending (reds). You can progress to letting both teams compete for the ball (first to ball wins possession for his team).
2. A goal in the first phase scores 1 point. A goal in the transition from defence to attack scores 2 points.
3. Recovering the ball in the transition from attack to defence scores 1 point.

COACHING TRANSITION PLAY

TACTICAL SITUATION 3

PEP GUARDIOLA TACTICS

Defensive Reactions When Regaining Possession Immediately Isn't Possible

**Analysis taken from 'FC Barcelona: A Tactical Analysis - Attacking'
(Athanasios Terzis 2011)**

Available to buy from SoccerTutor.com (paperback + eBook)

The analysis is based on recurring patterns of play. Once the same phase of play occurred a number of times (at least 10) the tactics would be decoded, with the positioning of each player on the pitch studied in great detail, including their body shape. Each individual movement with or without the ball was also recorded in detail. The analysis on the next page is an example of the team's tactics being used effectively.

The analysis is then used to create a full progressive session to coach this specific tactical situation.

Analysis taken from 'FC Barcelona: A Tactical Analysis - Attacking' (Athanasios Terzis)

Defensive Reactions When Regaining Possession Immediately Isn't Possible

The right winger (7) intercepts Iniesta's (8) pass

In this example, the right winger (7) intercepts Iniesta's attempted pass.

Because Iniesta (8) is unable to apply immediate pressure, Barcelona's defenders drop off in order to limit the space behind the defensive line. This movement gives Busquets time to move back and provide support to the defenders.

Iniesta (8) moves across to become first defender and keep ball near the sideline

Abidal (22) drops back to block pass towards No.9 before moving forward to contest No.7

Iniesta (8) becomes the first defender and tries to keep the ball carrier near the sideline.

Villa (7) moves towards the centre while Abidal (22) drops back to block off a possible pass towards No.9 who has made a diagonal run. Abidal (22) then pushes up to help double mark the ball carrier.

ASSESSMENT:

When immediate pressure is not possible, the defence drop deeper to cover the forwards' runs and give the team time to find balance again.

SESSION FOR THIS TACTICAL SITUATION (5 PRACTICES)
1. Defensive Reactions When Regaining Possession Immediately Isn't Possible in a 4 Zone SSG with 4 Goals

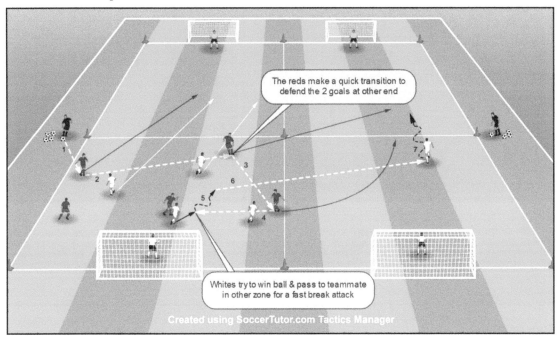

The reds make a quick transition to defend the 2 goals at other end

Whites try to win ball & pass to teammate in other zone for a fast break attack

Created using SoccerTutor.com Tactics Manager

Objective: To develop the transition from attack to defence when immediate pressure on the ball carrier isn't possible (tracking back and restoring balance).

Description

In a 40 x 40 yard area we split the pitch into 4 equal grids (2 attacking and 2 defensive grids for each team). We have a full size goal with a goalkeeper in each grid and work with 2 teams of 5 outfield players.

The practice starts with one team in possession (reds in diagram) with a 5 v 4 situation. The 5th player from the defending team (white) is positioned in the parallel grid (right side in the diagram), ready for the transition from defence to attack.

In the first grid, the reds try to score and the 4 white players attempt to win the ball and pass to their 5th player in the other grid. The white team then try to score in either of the 2 goals in their attacking half (top of diagram).

This forces all 5 players on the red team to make a very quick transition from attack to defence and prevent the whites from scoring. If the red team recover the ball successfully, you can restart the practice again in the following different ways:

1. Start again with the same objectives for both teams, but the attack starts from the parallel grid (right side in the diagram).

2. Start again with the team roles and objectives reversed (whites start in possession in their attacking half).

3. The practice continues until the ball goes out of play and both teams try score.

PROGRESSION

2. Defensive Reactions When Regaining Possession Immediately Isn't Possible in a Dynamic 2 Zone SSG

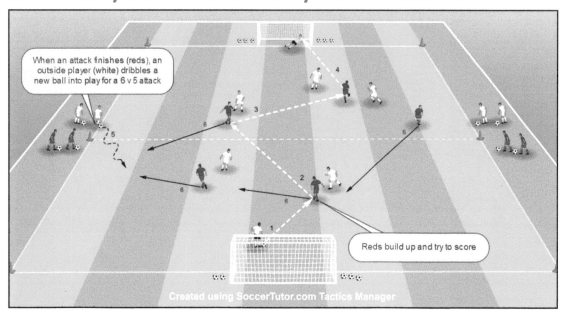

When an attack finishes (reds), an outside player (white) dribbles a new ball into play for a 6 v 5 attack

Reds build up and try to score

Description

In the same 40 x 40 yard area as the previous practice, we remove 2 of the goals and only have 2 grids (attacking and defensive), split by the halfway line. We play a normal 5 v 5 game starting from the goalkeeper, but we now have 4 extra players at the sides for each team (2 on each side as shown).

When a team finishes an attack (reds in diagram example), a player from the other team (whites) on the opposite side quickly runs inside with a new ball and attacks with a 6 v 5 situation.

The team which just finished their attack (reds) have a numerical disadvantage and must make a very quick transition from attack to defence, making sure to track back and take up effective defensive positions.

Rules

1. All players are either limited to 3 touches or have unlimited touches.
2. If the team in transition from defence to attack (whites in diagram) score a goal they get 1 point.
3. If the team in transition from attack to defence (reds in diagram) win the ball back, they score 1 point. If this happens, that team then have 12 seconds to score (2 points).

If a goal is scored or the ball goes out of play, start the practice from the beginning.

Coaching Points

1. Maintain good positions when your have possession, so you can react quickly and efficiently when possession is lost, thus reducing the risk.
2. There needs to be fast tracking back and support from other teammates to create a strong side to limit the options for the ball carrier.

3. Team Shape and Quickly Switching the Point of Defence in a 5 v 5 (+2) Tactical Practice

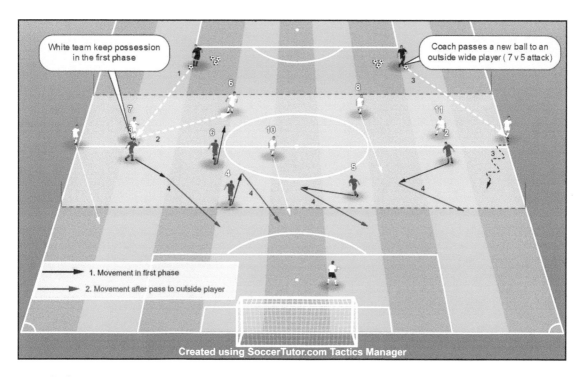

Description

Using a full pitch we create a middle zone and the red team have 2 centre backs (4 & 5), 2 full backs (2 & 3) and 1 defensive midfielder (6) from the 4-3-3 formation. We have 5 white midfield opponents in a 2-3 formation with 2 additional players outside at the sides on the halfway line.

The 5 white players start by keeping possession (without attacking the goal) and the 5 red defenders work together as a group and take up the correct positions in relation to where the ball is - one player presses the ball carrier and the others provide cover - they do not try to win the ball. The players wait for the coach to signal one of the 2 outside players who receives a pass from the coach and enters the pitch. The whites attack and try to score in a 7 v 5 situation. The red players must react quickly and collectively to defend the attack.

Variation: Change the red team to include 2 attacking midfielders, 2 wingers and 1 striker from the 4-3-3 formation against the white team with 2 centre backs, 2 full backs, a defensive midfielder and 2 extra side players.

Rules

1. From the moment the coach passes the second ball to the wide player, the white team have 10 seconds to finish their attack.
2. If the white team score they get 2 points. If the red team prevent them from scoring, they get 1 point.

Coaching Point: When in transition from attack to defence, the players need to drop off and give time for other players to recover back. This takes collective movement and shape - making sure not to leave big distances between each other. These defensive movements are displayed in the diagram.

PROGRESSION

4. Team Shape and Quickly Switching the Point of Defence in an 8 v 7 (+2) Practice

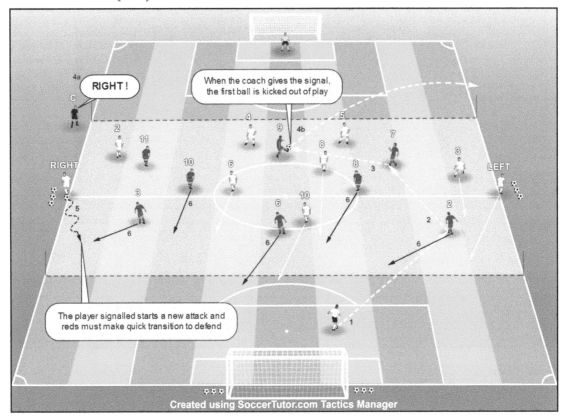

Description

In this progression of the previous practice, we increase the size of the middle zone. We now have 8 red outfield players versus 7 (+2) whites. The red team are in a 2-3-3 formation (from 4-3-3) with 2 full backs. The white team are in a 4-2-1 formation with 2 defensive midfielders (6 & 8) and 1 attacking midfielder (10). The white team also have 2 wingers who start outside on the halfway line with a ball.

The practice starts with the red goalkeeper and we play a normal game. When the coach calls out (right or left) the ball is kicked out of play and an outside white player ('RIGHT' in diagram) runs inside with the ball to launch a fast break attack on the red team's weak side. The red team make a quick transition from attack to defence with a numerical disadvantage (8 v 9) - they must react quickly and collectively, tracking back to defend their goal.

Rules

1. There are no zone restrictions after the first pass from the keeper but the zone helps us focus the play in the middle zone, before the players track back in the transition from attack to defence.
2. If the red team score a goal in the first phase of the game they get 1 point.
3. If the whites score with their fast break attack they get 2 points. If the reds recover the ball they get 1 point.
4. If the red team score after recovering the ball back in the second phase, they get 2 points.

PROGRESSION

5. Closing the Space in the Centre in a Tactical Transition Game

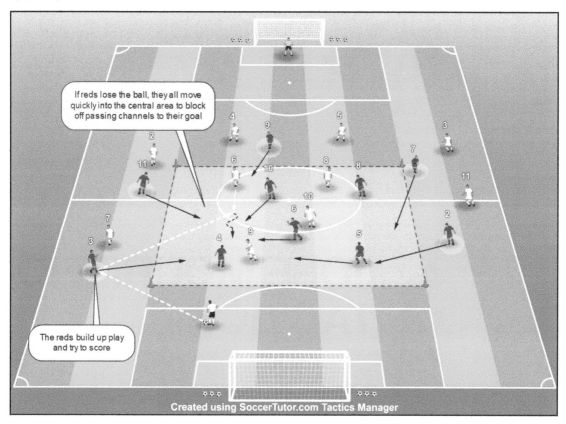

If reds lose the ball, they all move quickly into the central area to block off passing channels to their goal

The reds build up play and try to score

Created using SoccerTutor.com Tactics Manager

Description

In the final practice of this session, we mark out a 30 yard central area (the width of the penalty area) as shown in the diagram. There are no restrictions of movement/positioning in relation to the central area and we play a normal 11 v 11 game. The red team are in a 4-3-3 formation and the white team are in a 4-2-3-1 formation.

The practice starts with the goalkeeper as one team (reds) tries to build up play, create chances and score a goal. The defending team (whites) press collectively and try to win the ball.

If the red team lose the ball, the new objective is for all the red players to move quickly into the central area and block off the passing channels to goal. This forces their opponents (whites) to play back or into wide areas.

Coaching Points

1. There should be an immediate press of the opponent's new ball carrier from the nearest player. There also needs to be fast support from other teammates to create a numerical advantage around the ball zone.

2. The players in the centre of the pitch (centre backs, central midfielders) must be able to read the tactical situation and converge collectively, preventing the opposition from playing passes through the centre.

TACTICAL SITUATION 4

JOSE MOURINHO TACTICS

Team Shape and Collective Pressing When Possession is Lost

Analysis taken from 'Jose Mourinho's Real Madrid: A Tactical Analysis - Attacking in the 4-2-3-1' (Athanasios Terzis 2012)

Available to buy from SoccerTutor.com (paperback + eBook)

The analysis is based on recurring patterns of play. Once the same phase of play occurred a number of times (at least 10) the tactics would be decoded, with the positioning of each player on the pitch studied in great detail, including their body shape. Each individual movement with or without the ball was also recorded in detail. The analysis on the next page is an example of the team's tactics being used effectively.

The analysis is then used to create a full progressive session to coach this specific tactical situation.

Analysis taken from 'Jose Mourinho's Real Madrid: Attacking' (Athanasios Terzis)

Team Shape and Collective Pressing When Possession is Lost

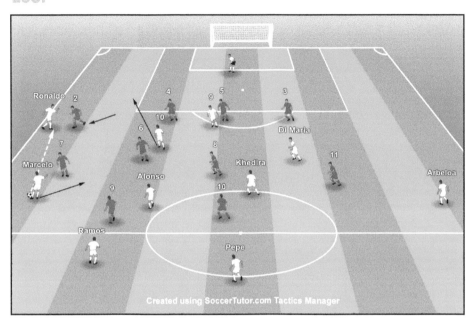

In this example, the left back Marcelo passes the ball to Ronaldo who is near the sideline and takes up a supporting position behind him.

The opposition right back (2) and winger (7) challenge Ronaldo and win the ball.

187

Immediate pressure on the ball carrier
- keeping the ball near the sideline

Created using SoccerTutor.com Tactics Manager

Marcelo (12) immediately puts pressure on the new ball carrier and Alonso (14) makes sure that the ball remains near the sideline by taking up a position towards the inside.

Ramos (4) marks No.9 and Pepe shifts to provide cover. Khedira (6) provides balance in midfield and Arbeloa moves towards the centre.

ASSESSMENT:

In other situations, when possession was lost in the centre and the Real Madrid players could not ensure the immediate regaining of possession, the midfielders made sure that the ball was forced out wide. This action gained time for the rest of the players to recover into effective defensive positions.

1. Team Shape and Collective Pressing in a Tactical Unopposed Practice

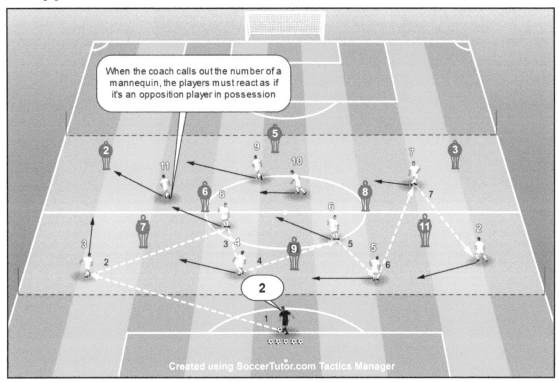

Objective: To work on collective team shape and movements in a quick transition from attack to defence in the middle zone.

Description

Using a full pitch we mark out a middle zone and place 8 numbered mannequins in the positions shown. We work with 10 players in a 4-2-3-1 formation. You can adjust the formation to suit your team's training.

The practice starts with one of the 4 defenders receiving from the coach and the team cooperate with fast combination play and basic tactical movements that we want to work on for this phase of the game.

The practice continues until the coach calls out a number of one of the mannequins. All of the players then make a transition from attack to defence as if that mannequin (opponent) now has possession of the ball.

Players need to move in relation to the mannequin's position, making sure to remain compact with short distances between each other. The nearest players should accelerate quickly towards the mannequin, as if they are closing down the ball carrier and blocking possible passing lanes.

The coach then passes a new ball into play and the practice continues with the same objective.

2. Team Shape and Collective Pressing in a Dynamic 11 v 11 Tactical Game

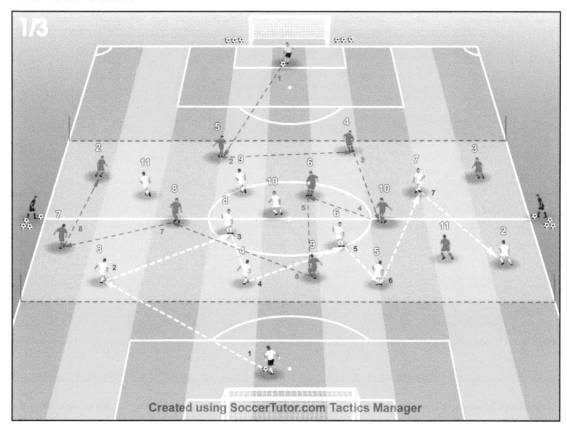

Created using SoccerTutor.com Tactics Manager

Description

Using the same middle zone as the last practice, we remove the mannequins and play 11 v 11. The blue team are in a 4-3-3 formation and the white team are in a 4-2-3-1 formation. You can adjust the formations to suit your team's training.

The practice starts with a goalkeeper's pass into the middle zone and both teams have a ball each. As in the last practice, the teams cooperate with fast combination play and basic tactical movements within the middle zone, that we want to work on for this phase of the game.

Coaching Points

1. The players should limit themselves to 2 touches (control and pass) but use 1 touch for backwards passes.
2. The focus should also be on maintaining good positions when we have possession in the middle zone, so we can react quickly and efficiently to losing the ball, thus reducing the risk in the transition to defence.

Phase 2 is explained on the next page...

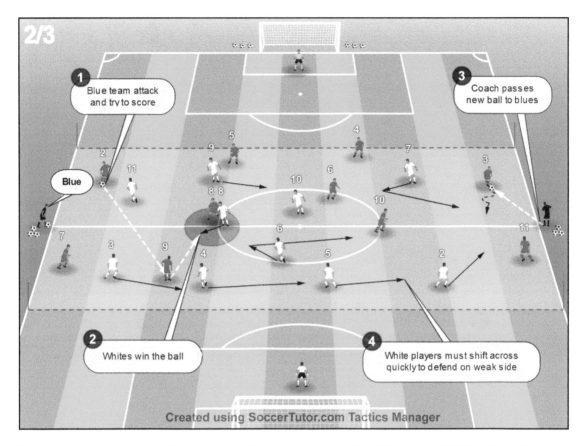

1 Blue team attack and try to score

3 Coach passes new ball to blues

Blue

2 Whites win the ball

4 White players must shift across quickly to defend on weak side

Created using SoccerTutor.com Tactics Manager

To begin phase 2, the coach calls out a colour (blue in example) and the white team's ball is kicked out of play. The blues then become the attacking team and the whites become the defending team.

1. The blue team attack and trying to score.

2. The white team must make a quick transition from attack to defence, trying to reduce the space and time for the blue team, force a bad decision and win the ball. In the diagram example, the white No.8 is able to win the ball.

3. If the blues lose the ball, finish their attack or the ball goes out of play, the other coach passes a new ball into a blue player on the other side and the blues start another attack on the weak side of their opponents.

4. The white team have to make a transition from attack to defence again and quickly get back into position.

Coaching Points

1. The white team's players must shift across collectively, making sure to keep short distances between each other.

2. One player should close down the ball carrier, while the other players mark their opponents tightly and block the direct passing lanes towards goal.

Phase 3 is explained on the next page...

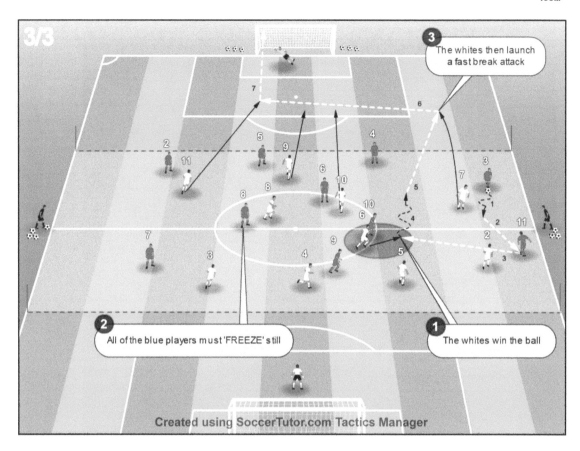

We start phase 3 with the blue team attacking and trying to score. If the white team win the ball back again (white No.6 wins the ball in the diagram example), the blue players must all 'freeze' and stay in their positions. The whites launch a fast break attack, aware of the positioning of their opponents.

When the white team's fast break attack is finished, they must run very quickly back to the middle zone and into their starting positions, ready for the practice to start again from phase 1 (page 190).

Rules

1. Once the coach passes a new ball into play, that team have a limited time to finish their attack.
2. If a team scores with their first attack, the goal counts double.

Coaching Points

1. If the white team win the ball, they should then play the ball quickly into space (in relation to the positioning of the opposition) and in behind the defensive line.
2. The players should make fast supporting runs, which are well timed into the penalty area.

CHAPTER 10

TRANSITION FROM ATTACK TO DEFENCE IN THE HIGH ZONE

TRANSITION FROM ATTACK TO DEFENCE IN THE HIGH ZONE

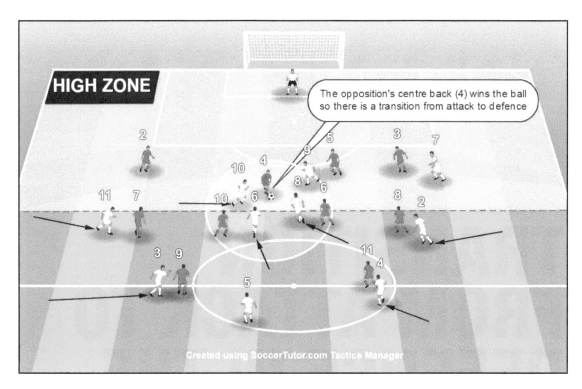

For this book, we have divided the chapters by which zone the transition starts in. There are 3 zones:

1. **Low Zone**

2. **Middle Zone**

3. High Zone

This diagram shows an example of a team losing the ball in the high zone. In this situation, the red team's centre back (4) wins the ball. It is important that pressure is applied to the new ball carrier immediately, before he is able to get his head up to dribble or pass forward. We want to create a numerical superiority in and around the ball zone. We also have many players in the opposition half and need to prevent an early long ball in behind our defensive line, where there is lots of space to run into.

The 3 central midfielders (6, 8 &10) close down the ball carrier immediately and also block the potential passes towards the red No.6 and No.10 respectively.

All of the other players move inside to create a congested central zone and mark their opponents tightly. This closes the space in which the opposition can play and prevents them from playing the ball wide or utilising the space in behind.

The players need to work together as a full team, because if just one doesn't react quickly enough, the opposition could have an easy passing opportunity in behind with a goal scoring chance. If it is done effectively, the team will recover possession.

Players need to also be aware and have quick reactions to track back in case the first press of the ball is not effective. They need to prevent a numerical disadvantage from occurring during the opposition's potential counter attack.

COACHING TRANSITION PLAY

What is the Tactical Situation?

- We have many players in the opposition half.

- We have short distances between the lines.

- There are many opposition players in this half.

- We have a lot of space in behind our defensive line as we are high up the pitch.

- There is a short distance to the opponent's goal.

- The opposition have 1-2 players level with or near our defensive line.

- We have an equality of numbers and many potential 1 v 1 battle situations.

- The counter attacks from the opposition take 8-12 seconds on average.

What Objectives Should We Have?

- To pass very quickly from attack to defence in the area that we lose the ball, limiting the time and space for our opponents, marking players around the ball zone very tightly and blocking off potential passing lanes.

- To quickly press the player with the ball to avoid them passing or dribbling forward and forcing them to play under pressure of time and space.

- The basic aim is to win the ball or to force our opponents into making a wrong decision.

- Avoid making fouls when the opponent is under pressure of time and space and has no solutions. If a foul is committed, it stops the press and solves the problem for our opponents.

- To avoid the opposition playing long balls in behind our defensive line, which would neutralise the many players we have high up the pitch.

- To create a numerical superiority in and around the ball area and create a strong side.

- Players need to be aware and have quick reactions to track back in case the first press of the ball is not effective. They need to prevent a numerical disadvantage from occurring at the back from the opposition's counter attack.

What Practices/Sessions Can We Create for this Tactical Situation?

- High intensity possession and transition practices which force our players to react very quickly and effectively when we lose the ball in the high zone and in tight areas of the pitch.

- Practices focussed on awareness, tactical movements, decision making and high energy when possession is lost high up the pitch.

- Practices with organised attacks and tactical movements in the opposition's half against organised defences with many players behind the ball. The focus is on fast and effective transitions from attack to defence, but we need to be aware that it depends on our formation (strengths and weaknesses) against the formation of our opponents.

TACTICAL SITUATION 1

JOSE MOURINHO TACTICS

Losing Possession Near the Opposition's Penalty Area (1)

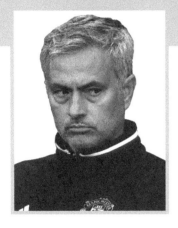

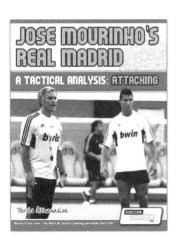

Analysis taken from 'Jose Mourinho's Real Madrid: A Tactical Analysis - Attacking in the 4-2-3-1' (Athanasios Terzis 2012)

Available to buy from SoccerTutor.com (paperback + eBook)

The analysis is based on recurring patterns of play. Once the same phase of play occurred a number of times (at least 10) the tactics would be decoded, with the positioning of each player on the pitch studied in great detail, including their body shape. Each individual movement with or without the ball was also recorded in detail. The analysis on the next page is an example of the team's tactics being used effectively.

The analysis is then used to create a full progressive session to coach this specific tactical situation.

Analysis taken from 'Jose Mourinho's Real Madrid: Attacking' (Athanasios Terzis)

Losing Possession Near the Opposition's Penalty Area (1)

In this situation, the defensive midfielder Khedira (6) has switched the play with a long pass out to the flank where the left back Marcelo (12) has made a forward run into the space.

Marcelo receives and dribbles the ball down the flank but is under pressure from the right back (2).

The right back (2) wins the ball and passes to No.7. Alonso (14) and Ozil apply pressure immediately.

Khedira (6) marks No.9 and there is a numerical advantage around the ball zone, so it is likely that Madrid will win the ball back quickly.

There is a superiority in numbers in defence in case the opposition manage to play through the pressure.

1. Possession and Ball Recovery in a 3 Team 2 Zone Game

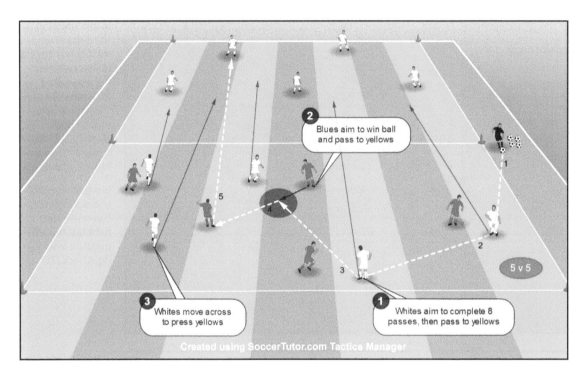

2 — Blues aim to win ball and pass to yellows

3 — Whites move across to press yellows

1 — Whites aim to complete 8 passes, then pass to yellows

5 v 5

Created using SoccerTutor.com Tactics Manager

Description

In 30 x 40 yard area we divide the pitch into 2 equal zones. We have 3 teams with 5 players each. The practice starts in one zone with 2 teams - the third team (yellows) wait in the opposite zone.

One team starts with possession (whites in diagram example) and play 5 v 5 against the blue team. The objective for the team in possession is to complete 8 consecutive passes and then pass the ball to the third team (yellows) in the opposite zone. The blue team would then have to run quickly across to apply pressure to the yellows.

The objective for the blue team is to apply pressure, win the ball and pass the ball to the yellow team themselves (as shown in diagram). The white team must then move across to defend and the practice continues in the same way with the yellows in possession, trying to complete 8 passes before passing to the blues.

When a team loses the ball (whites) and the opposition (blues) pass into the other zone, they must make a quick transition from attack to defence and run across to apply pressure and try to recover the ball as soon as possible. If the white team are then able to recover the ball from the yellow team in the other grid, they then pass back across to the blue team and the yellows then must move across to pressure the blues.

Rules

1. All players have unlimited touches / All players are limited to 3 touches.
2. If any team wins the ball in the transition from attack to defence within 8 seconds and then successfully passes the ball to the team in the other zone, they score 1 point.

2. Possession and Transition Play in a Position Specific 2 Zone Game

Blues try to win ball & pass to No.5 (players move across with team roles reversed)

Whites try to complete 6-8 passes (1 point)

Created using SoccerTutor.com Tactics Manager

Objective: To work on pressing high and quick transitions from attack to defence.

Description

In a 35 x 45 yard area, we divide the pitch into 2 equal zones. We have the exact same objectives as the previous practice but we now play 7 v 7 with the teams in specific formations.

The white team are in a 4-3 formation with 4 players positioned outside of the area (the back 4) and 3 players inside one zone (3 central midfielders). The other team (blues) have 6 players inside one zone in a 2-3-1 formation (2 defensive midfielders, 1 attacking midfielder, 2 wingers and 1 striker) - the seventh player (No.5) is on the end line of the opposite zone as shown.

The practice starts with one team in possession (whites in diagram) in one zone. The white team keep possession, trying to complete 6-8 passes (1 point) and the blues apply pressure, trying to win the ball before passing to their teammate in the other zone. If this happens, the blue players move across quickly to keep possession in the other zone with the same 4 outside/3 inside situation as the white team had.

The white team make a quick transition from attack to defence, but 1 player (No.5) stays in the outside position on the bottom end line. If the white team win the ball back in the other zone, they then pass to this player. The practice is continuous.

Rule: All players have unlimited touches / All players are limited to 3 touches.

3. Fast Reactions to Recover the Ball in a Dynamic 7 v 7 Game

If blues win ball, they pass to GK. Whites must then make a fast transition from attack to defence.

Whites aim to keep possession

Objective: To develop quick reactions when possession is lost and recover the ball as soon as possible.

Description

In a 20 x 40 yard area we divide the pitch into 2 equal zones and play a 7 v 7 game. The practice starts with a keeper and one team (whites in example) in their half, keeping possession of the ball.

The other team (blues) try to win the ball and then pass it back to their goalkeeper. They then move across and receive a pass from their goalkeeper and try to keep possession in their half. The white team have the following aims when making a quick transition from attack to defence:

1. At first they try to stop the blue team passing to their goalkeeper.

2. If the blues do manage to pass to their keeper, the white team move very quickly into the other zone and press the opposition to recover the ball as soon as they can and pass it back to their keeper in their half.

Both teams have the same objectives and the situation/roles change continuously.

Rule: All players have unlimited touches / All players are limited to 3 touches.

4. Pressing High Up the Pitch to Recover Possession in a 3 Zone Tactical Game

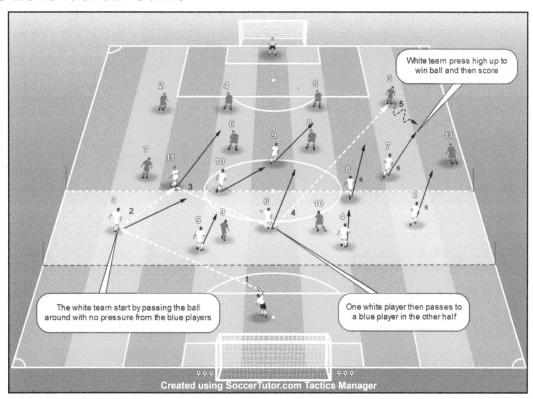

White team press high up to win ball and then score

The white team start by passing the ball around with no pressure from the blue players

One white player then passes to a blue player in the other half

Created using SoccerTutor.com Tactics Manager

Description

Using a full pitch we create a 'white zone' from the halfway line and 20 yards back, as shown in the diagram. We play 11 v 11 with the white team in a 4-3-3 or 4-2-3-1 formation and the blue team in a 4-4-2 formation.

The practice starts with the goalkeeper's pass into the white zone and the whites pass the ball around without pressure from their blue opponents. At any point, a white player can choose to pass to one of the blue players in the other half. At this point there are no longer any zone restrictions and the white players make a quick transition from attack to defence and apply a high press (as a team) in the high zone of the pitch.

The blue team's objectives:

1. If the blue team receive a pass in behind the white defensive line (final zone with goalkeeper past the blue dashed line), they score 1 point.
2. If the blue team score a goal they get 2 points.

The white team's objectives:

1. If the white team recover the ball and score a goal they get 1 point.
2. If the white team recover the ball within 8 seconds and then score a goal, they get 2 points.

After a few repetitions, reverse the team roles and objectives.

PROGRESSION

5. Pressing High Up the Pitch to Recover Possession in an 11 v 11 Game

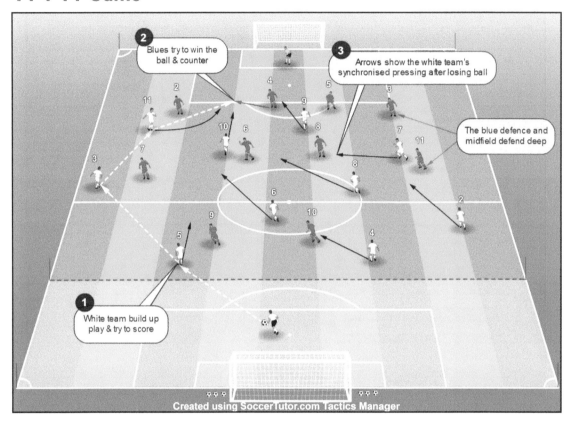

Description

In this progression of the previous practice, we simply merge the 2 zones and play a normal 11 v 11 game. The practice always starts with the white team's goalkeeper. We still mark out the final zone, as the blue team can score a point by receiving a pass in behind the white defensive line within this zone.

The blue team's defence and midfield defend deep in their low zone. The white team build up play from the back and try to score. The blue team keep compact, try to win the ball and then score with a counter attack.

If the white team lose the ball, they apply quick and synchronised pressing of the ball and the area around it (as shown by the black movement arrows). Their main objective is to make a quick transition from attack to defence, preventing their opponents from making a successful counter attack and recovering the ball as soon as possible. They then look to score themselves. The same objectives and points scoring apply from the previous practice.

Coaching Points

1. Limit the time and space, mark players around the ball zone very tightly and block off potential passing lanes.
2. Stop any long balls in behind the defensive line, which would neutralise the many players high up the pitch.

COACHING TRANSITION PLAY

TACTICAL SITUATION 2

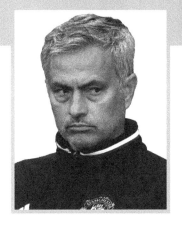

JOSE MOURINHO TACTICS

Losing Possession Near the Opposition's Penalty Area (2)

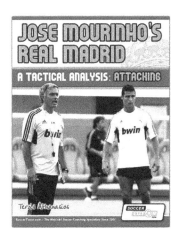

Analysis taken from 'Jose Mourinho's Real Madrid: A Tactical Analysis - Attacking in the 4-2-3-1' (Athanasios Terzis 2012)

Available to buy from SoccerTutor.com (paperback + eBook)

The analysis is based on recurring patterns of play. Once the same phase of play occurred a number of times (at least 10) the tactics would be decoded, with the positioning of each player on the pitch studied in great detail, including their body shape. Each individual movement with or without the ball was also recorded in detail. The analysis on the next page is an example of the team's tactics being used effectively.

The analysis is then used to create a full progressive session to coach this specific tactical situation.

Analysis taken from 'Jose Mourinho's Real Madrid: Attacking' (Athanasios Terzis)

Losing Possession Near the Opposition's Penalty Area (2)

In this example Real Madrid have switched play from the right side to Ronaldo high up on the left flank.

Ronaldo tries to beat the right back (2) and get to the byline.

The Madrid left back Marcelo (12) is the safety player and must react quickly if possession is lost.

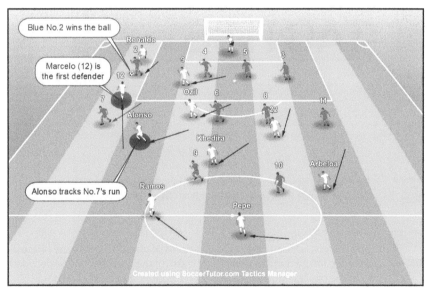

No.2 wins the ball. Marcelo (12) applies pressure immediately and Alonso (14) tracks No.7's run.

Benzema (9) and Ozil (10) shift towards the left to block a possible pass towards the centre. Khedira (6) moves to provide balance after Alonso's extensive shift. Ramos has no player to mark so moves towards the strong side in case a long pass is played. Arbeloa moves back and ensures superiority in numbers for Real.

ASSESSMENT:

When possession was lost high up the pitch, the Real Madrid player who took over the role of the first defender sought to regain the ball immediately. If the immediate regaining of possession was not possible, the main aim would be to keep the ball near the sideline to allow time for the rest of the players to recover and take up effective defensive positions.

1. Quick and Efficient Reactions in the Transition from Attack to Defence in a Dynamic Game

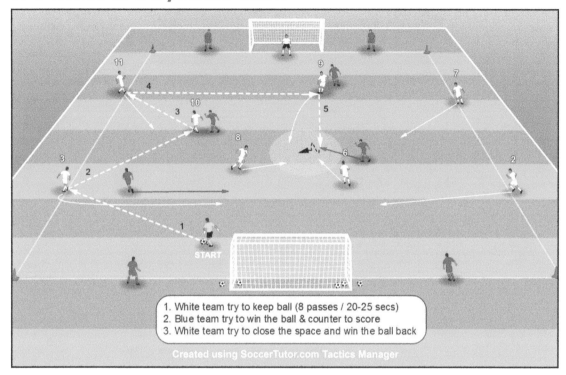

1. White team try to keep ball (8 passes / 20-25 secs)
2. Blue team try to win the ball & counter to score
3. White team try to close the space and win the ball back

Created using SoccerTutor.com Tactics Manager

Description

In a 25 x 25 yard area, we have 2 full size goals with goalkeepers and 2 teams of 8 players. One team (whites) have 4 outside players at the sides of the pitch (full backs and wingers) and the other team (blues) have 4 outside players on the 2 end lines either side of the goals, as shown.

The white team's keeper starts and the first objective is to keep the ball for as long is possible without trying to score. They score 1 point for completing 8 passes and 2 points if they keep the ball for 20-25 seconds. If they lose the ball, they must make a quick transition from attack to defence - pressing the ball, closing the space around the ball and limiting the choices for the blues. The objective for the blue team is to win the ball and try to score in either of the 2 goals.

When the whites have the ball, they should *OPEN* the pitch (making the area big to keep possession) and when they lose the ball, they should *CLOSE* it (denying space and time to the opposition). Change the team roles often.

Rules

1. The white players are limited to 2 or 3 touches. The blue inside players have unlimited touches. All of the outside players are limited to 1 or 2 touches.
2. The blue team get 1 point for scoring a goal. If the whites recover the ball within 6 seconds they get 1 point.
3. The white outside players are allowed to enter the pitch for the transition from attack to defence.
4. The blue outside players are not allowed to enter the pitch at any point and cannot score a goal.

205

2. High Press to Block Off Forward Options for the Opposition in a Small Sided Game with Cone Gates

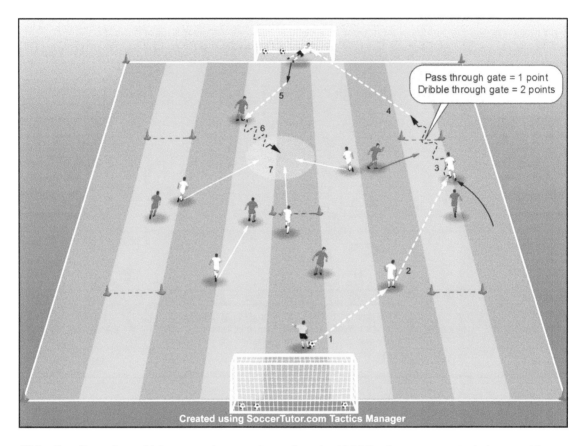

Pass through gate = 1 point
Dribble through gate = 2 points

Created using SoccerTutor.com Tactics Manager

Objective: To work on a high press and prevent forward passing/dribbling from opponents during transitions.

Description

In a 30 x 40 yard area we have 2 full size goals with goalkeepers and we create 5 small cone gates in the positions shown. We play 6 v 6 with the teams in a 2-3-1 (or 3-3) formation and play a high intensity small sided game with the emphasis on the transition from attack to defence. The game starts with a goalkeeper and one team in possession (whites in diagram example) with the following objectives:

- To pass a ball from one teammate to another through a cone gate (1 point).
- To dribble the ball through a cone gate (2 points) - this is shown in the diagram.
- To score a goal (3 points).

All these different opportunities to score make the defending team apply intense pressure to the ball, especially to the ball carrier and in and around the ball zone. This is done to limit the choices of the ball carrier and force a mistake - ultimately preventing the opposition from scoring any points.

COACHING TRANSITION PLAY

VARIATION

3. High Press to Block Off Forward Passing Options for the Opposition in a SSG with No Goalkeeper

Objective: To develop a quick high press in the transition from attack to defence.

Description

In this variation of the previous practice, we remove the white team's goalkeeper and the cone gates. The white team start in possession with one player dribbling the ball into play, and try to score. If they lose possession, they must apply pressure to the new ball carrier immediately, converge together around the ball area, limit the time/space for their opponents and prevent them from shooting or passing to a teammate in a better position.

The empty goal forces the players and the team to make very quick adjustments and synchronise their reactions when they lose the ball. If they don't, their opponents could score easily into the open net. When the ball goes out, the team without a goalkeeper always starts in possession. After some repetitions, change the team roles.

Rules

1. The white team have unlimited touches and the blue team are limited to 2 or 3 touches.
2. If the blue team score a goal they get 1 point. If the white team score a goal they get 2 points.
3. If the white team recover the ball within 6 seconds of losing it, they get 1 point.

4. High Press After Losing Possession Near the Opposition Penalty Area in a 3 Zone Game

If white team lose ball in zone 3, they apply a high press

Description

For this 11 v 11 game, we create 3 zones - a low zone (15 yards), a middle zone (25 yards) and a high zone (40 yards). Players can move freely across all zones. The whites are in a 4-2-3-1 formation and the blues are in a 4-4-2. We play a normal game starting from the goalkeeper, but the white team have a specific objective. If they lose the ball, they must make a quick transition from attack to defence, with synchronised reactions from all players.

If they lose the ball in the high zone (3) they must apply high pressure to the ball carrier immediately, limit their opponent's options to play forward and force them into making a wrong decision so that the ball can be recovered quickly. This example is shown in the diagram.

If they lose the ball in the middle zone (2), all players must quickly converge together around the ball area with players ahead of the ball tracking back and players behind the ball pushing up - this is to prevent the opposition from being able to pass into the next and final zone (1).

Rules

1. A white goal scores 1 point and if they recover the ball within 6 seconds of losing it, they get 1 point.
2. If the blue team pass the ball into zone 1 (and receive successfully) they get 1 point and if they score a goal, they get 2 points.
3. If the white players in front of the ball in zone 3 (when possession is lost) do not return to the middle zone (2) within 6 seconds of the ball being played in there, the blues get 1 point.

5. Recovering the Ball Within 6 Seconds of Losing Possession in an 11 v 11 Game

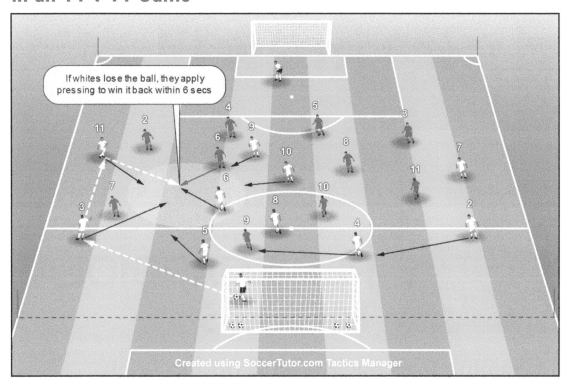

If whites lose the ball, they apply pressing to win it back within 6 secs

Description

In this variation and final practice of the session, we remove the 3 zones and play a normal 11 v 11 game in the same area.

The objective for the white team is again on a quick transition from attack to defence. The game starts with the white goalkeeper and the white team in possession, building up play and trying to score. The blue team defend, try to win the ball and then launch a counter attack to score themselves. If the white team lose the ball at any time (anywhere on the pitch), their aim is to recover the ball within 6 seconds.

Rules

1. A white goal scores 1 point.
2. If the white team recover the ball within 6 seconds of losing it, they get 1 point.
3. A blue goal scores 2 points.

Coaching Points

1. In the transition from attack to defence, create a numerical superiority in and around the ball area and create a strong side.
2. Avoid fouls when the opponent is under pressure of time and space and has no solutions. If a foul is committed, it stops the press and solves the problem for the opposition.

TACTICAL SITUATION 3

PEP GUARDIOLA TACTICS

Regaining Possession High Up the Pitch

**Analysis taken from 'FC Barcelona: A Tactical Analysis - Attacking'
(Athanasios Terzis 2011)**

Available to buy from SoccerTutor.com (paperback + eBook)

The analysis is based on recurring patterns of play. Once the same phase of play occurred a number of times (at least 10) the tactics would be decoded, with the positioning of each player on the pitch studied in great detail, including their body shape. Each individual movement with or without the ball was also recorded in detail. The analysis on the next page is an example of the team's tactics being used effectively.

The analysis is then used to create a full progressive session to coach this specific tactical situation.

Analysis taken from 'FC Barcelona: A Tactical Analysis - Attacking' (Athanasios Terzis)

Regaining Possession High Up the Pitch

This is an example of Pep Guardiola's team losing possession high up the pitch and then regaining it very quickly with intense and collective pressing.

Busquets (16) attempts a forward pass to Messi (10), but the opposition's centre back (4) reads it well and intercepts the ball near the edge of the penalty area.

After the ball is intercepted by the opposition centre back (4), Xavi (6) and Iniesta (8) move to double mark the him, while Busquets (16) moves to prevent a possible pass towards No.10.

Abidal and Pique (3) mark the 2 forwards closely in order to block off possible passes directed towards them. The whole team converge to close the space, which would result in Barca recovering the ball.

SESSION FOR THIS TACTICAL SITUATION (5 PRACTICES)
1. High Pressing and Blocking Forward Passes in a Small Sided Game with Support Players

Red team press high up collectively to stop opponents playing into their half where there is a numerical advantage

Created using SoccerTutor.com Tactics Manager

Objective: We work on pressing high and preventing long or short passes through the press.

Description

In a 40 x 50 yard area we divide the pitch into 2 halves (40 x 25 yards each). The players can move freely across both halves. We have 2 full size goals with goalkeepers and each team has 9 outfield players.

Each team has 5 players inside the area in a 2-3 formation with an additional 4 support players in the opposition's half (in the positions shown in the diagram).

The practice starts from the goalkeeper with one team in possession (whites in diagram example) and the objective is to attack, move the ball into the attacking half and score. The attack must include at least 1 pass to a support player before a goal can be scored.

As the white team have a numerical advantage in their attacking half, this forces the defending team (reds) to press high and try to win the ball high up the pitch to block forward passes. This limits the options for the ball carrier, puts him under pressure and forces him into making wrong decisions and losing possession for his team.

PROGRESSION

2. High Press and Transition to Defence in a Position Specific 2 Zone Game

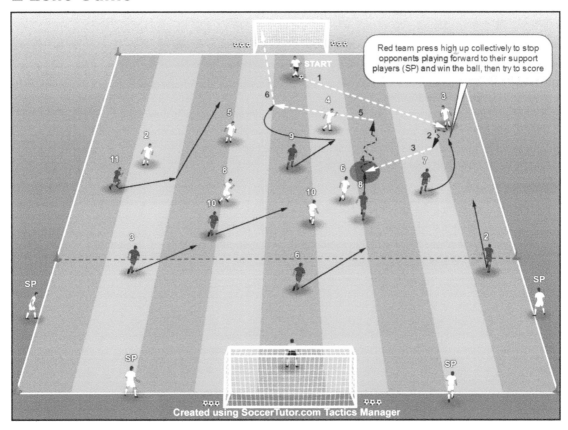

Objective: We work on pressing high and preventing long or short passes through the press.

Description

In this progression of the previous practice, we reduce the size of the low zone to 40 x 15 yards. The red team now have 8 outfield players all inside the area in a 2-3-3 formation (from 4-3-3). The white team have 7 outfield players inside the area in a 4-2-1 formation and 4 outside support players in the positions shown.

Scenario 1 (Diagram)

The practice starts with the white team's goalkeeper - as soon as he passes the ball, the red team start a high press (all players move into the high zone) with the objective to block passes from the inside players to the outside players and win the ball.

If the red team win the ball, their second objective is to try to score. If the red team lose the ball in this phase, they must remain in the high zone and make a quick transition from attack to defence. They revert back to the first objective - high press, block passes from the inside players to the outside players and win the ball.

After the attack is finished or the ball goes out of play, the practice starts again with the white team's goalkeeper.

Scenario 2

The practice starts with the red team's goalkeeper and the red team try to score a goal. If they lose possession, they must make a quick transition from attack to defence - their objective is to close down the ball carrier immediately, block passes from the inside players to the outside players and win the ball.

Progression: If you want to make the practice more difficult for the red team, you can remove the 2 red full backs (2 & 3).

Rules

1. All players have unlimited touches.
2. The white inside players have unlimited touches, the white outside players are limited to 1 or 2 touches and the red players have 2-3 touches.
3. When a white inside player passes to an outside support player successfully, they score 1 point.
4. If the white team score a goal they get 2 points (the outside players are not allowed to score).
5. If the red team regain possession after losing the ball, they get 1 point.
6. If the red team score a goal they get 2 points.

Coaching Points

1. Press high up, limiting the time and space for our opponents.
2. Mark players around the ball zone very tightly and block off potential passing lanes.
3. Quickly press the player with the ball to avoid them passing or dribbling forward, forcing them to play under pressure of time and space.

PROGRESSION

3. Regaining Possession High Up the Pitch in a 9 v 9 (+4) Game with 6 Goals

Objective: To develop the transition from attack to defence in the high zone of the pitch.

Description

Using half a pitch, we have 2 full size goals at either end and 4 small goals in the positions shown. These goals help develop the transition from attack to defence as you have to close the player very quickly to prevent them from scoring easily. The red team are in a 2-3-3 formation (from 4-3-3) and the white team are in a 4-2-1 formation. We also have 4 white support players (SP) in the positions shown.

The practice always starts with the red team's goalkeeper and the reds try to build up play and score in the full size goal past the goalkeeper (1 point). If the red team lose possession, their second objective is to apply immediate high pressure on the ball to prevent their opponents (white team) from passing to one of the support players or scoring a goal in any of the 4 small goals, or the full size goal at the other end.

Different Rules

1. All players have unlimited touches but the white outside support players are limited to 1 or 2 touches.
2. The red players are limited to 2-3 touches, the white players have unlimited touches and the support players are limited to 1 or 2 touches.
3. If the red team regain possession after losing the ball, they get 1 point.
4. If the red team score a goal they get 2 points.
5. If a white inside player passes to an outside support player successfully, the white team score 1 point.
6. If the white team score in a small goal they get 2 points. If they score in the full size goal they get 3 points (the support players are not allowed to score goals).

PROGRESSION

4. Regaining Possession High Up the Pitch in a Position Specific 2 Zone Game with Support Players (1)

Reds build up play and try to score

If reds lose the ball, they apply immediate high press

White team aim to win ball, pass to support players and attack

Created using SoccerTutor.com Tactics Manager

Description

In this progression of the previous practice, we have one zone which is half of a full pitch and a second zone which is the area between the halfway line and the edge of the penalty box.

The red team (2-3-3) always start with possession in the high zone (first pass from goalkeeper into the high zone) and try to score a goal against the white team's compact and deep 4-4 formation. In the low zone we have 2 blue support players for the white team. If the red team lose possession, their second objective is to apply immediate high pressure on the ball to prevent their opponents (whites) from passing to one of the blue support players in the other zone.

If a white player is able to pass to a blue support player, the white players can then run forward to receive a pass, trying to score with a quick counter attack. All of the red players must then track back quickly to defend their goal. Once the whites win the ball, all players can move across to the other zone to defend/attack.

Rules

1. The blue support players must remain within their zone at all times and are limited to 1 or 2 touches.
2. The blue support players are not allowed to score and can only pass to the white players once they have entered their zone.
3. All of the same rules from the previous practice still apply.

VARIATION

5. Regaining Possession High Up the Pitch in a Position Specific 2 Zone Game with Support Players (2)

Blue support players now play with both teams as CB or forward

Created using SoccerTutor.com Tactics Manager

Description

In this variation of the previous practice, the only change is that the blue support players now work with both teams - whichever team is in possession.

When the red team are in possession we have an 11 v 9 game, as the blue support players take up the roles of the 2 centre backs (4 & 5) in a 4-3-3 formation. They stay within the low zone but are available for passes back to maintain possession.

When the white team are in possession we have an 11 v 9 game in favour of the whites, as the blue support players take up the roles of the 2 forwards (9 & 10) in a 4-4-2 or 4-4-1-1 formation.

The rules are exactly the same as in the previous practice.

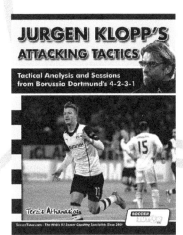

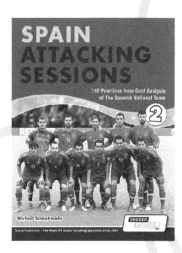

Lightning Source UK Ltd.
Milton Keynes UK
UKHW050843070620
364511UK00003B/28